IT MAKES SENSE
The handbook to believing

IT MAKES SENSE
An su@goldhill product published by Scripture Union, 207–209 Queensway, Bletchley, MK2 2EB, England. This imprint is specially created to bring the ministry of Gold Hill Baptist Church to a wider audience.

&Scripture Union is an international Christian charity working with churches in more than 130 countries providing resources to bring the good news about Jesus Christ to children, young people and families – and to encourage them to develop spiritually through the Bible and prayer. As well as our network of volunteers, staff and associates who run holidays, church-based events and school Christian groups, we produce a wide range of publications and support those who use our resources through training programmes.

Email: info@scriptureunion.org.uk   Internet: www.scriptureunion.org.uk

Scripture Union Australia
Locked Bag 2, Central Coast Business Centre, NSW 2252 222 www.su.org.au

Gold Hill: Gold Hill is a Baptist Church and member of the Evangelical Alliance. Their mission statement is: *Equipping God's people, Serving God's Son, Reaching God's World.* The church meets at Gold Hill Common East, Chalfont St Peter, SL9 9DG. Stephen Gaukroger is the senior pastor.

Email: office@goldhill.org.uk   Internet: www.goldhill.org.uk

Scripture quotations are taken from the Contemporary English Version (CEV) published by The Bible Societies/ HarperCollins Publishers, © 1991, 1995 American Bible Society. The poem *Match of the Day* by Gordon Bailey and quoted in Chapter 10 is from *Plastic World* published by STL (1971) and used with permission.

British Library Cataloguing-in-Publication Data: a catalogue record for this book is available from the British Library.

Cover design by Aricot Vert of Fleet, Hampshire
Illustrations by Susan Rann
Internal design and typesetting by Servis Filmsetting Ltd of Manchester
Printed and bound by Creative Print and Design (Wales) Ebbw Vale

Scripture Union
USING THE BIBLE TO INSPIRE CHILDREN, YOUNG PEOPLE AND ADULTS TO KNOW GOD

IT MAKES SENSE

The handbook to believing

Stephen Gaukroger

For
JLM, BJ, CE and SR, whom I love

Contents

About the author

Stephen Gaukroger, born in Sheffield, was converted, baptised and called to the pastoral ministry while attending Carey Baptist church in Preston, Lancashire. Following training at Spurgeon's College, he spent a year on the staff of First Baptist Church, Dallas, Texas.

Currently he is Senior Minister at Gold Hill Baptist Church, one of the largest churches in England. He is a prolific author with a popular style. Many of his 19 books have been widely translated.

Stephen is regarded as one of the most significant leaders of his generation in the UK. He has a clear grasp of postmodern culture and addresses its challenges with an unquestioned commitment to Scripture.

He regards mission/evangelism as a key priority for the Church, both locally and nationally, and it is this reality which drives his leadership. Until recently Stephen was a leader of Spring Harvest, widely recognised as the most influential Christian teaching event of the last 25 years. He was President of the Baptist Union of Great Britain from 1994–5, and now serves on the Council of Spurgeon's College, chairs the European Board of the Luis Palau Evangelistic Association and also chairs the Council of Reference of the European branch of Jews for Jesus.

He is married to Janet, who is very involved with worship and with Christian work among under fives, and they have three children.

1

Can I really believe in God?

This is the big question. Everything else depends on the answer. Does God exist, or are Christians just imagining the whole thing? And if we do end up proving that God is a figment of our imagination, shouldn't somebody let him know?

Some people today give the impression that thinking people don't believe in God any more; he has been relegated to the same place as the Tooth Fairy and Father Christmas (though sometimes it seems Father Christmas gets a higher rating!). God comes into the category of 'things we used to believe but have now grown out of'!

Well, are Christians just uninformed, gullible people? Or is this perhaps the condition of the atheist or the agnostic?

Atheism

An atheist says that God does not exist. Let's make some observations about this statement.

It is a statement of faith

Yes, it really is. The atheist can offer no logical, irrefutable proof for his case. He may draw on certain philosophical arguments, personal experiences or 'informed opinion' – but in the end none of this will be conclusive proof. Not only that, the very nature of his case is difficult: it is always harder to establish clearly what is *not* than to establish what is.

Say, for example, I call downstairs to my wife in the morning, 'I can't find my blue socks!'

She says, 'They're in the spare room.'

I look for a few moments, then yell, 'No, they're not!'

'Yes, they are,' she replies.

It's much easier for her to prove her case. If she comes upstairs and finds my socks, she was right. Even if she can't find them straight away, she may still be right if they are found later. To prove *my* case I have to search every inch of the room, leaving absolutely no space unexplored. She will only have been proved wrong when I have done all this. Similarly, atheism can only be proved right if every single scrap of information is ferreted out and analysed for traces of God.

An impossible task! Not even the most arrogant of human beings would claim to know everything. Yet without this knowledge how can the atheist say *for certain* that God does not exist? The statement 'There is no God' has 'Case unproved' stamped across it.

It is insecure

Being an atheist means living every day with the possibility that evidence will come to light which will prove you wrong. Back to my socks. Every moment of the search could prove me wrong; every moment could prove my wife right. I can only be right at the end of a long search; she could be right any time during the search.

This is a trivial illustration but, if the outcome of our search were crucial, my every moment would be filled with dread at being proved wrong; hers would be filled with the hope of being proved right. So, logically speaking, an atheist is never secure until he or she has explored all the options. George Bernard Shaw, atheist playwright whose work inspired *My Fair Lady*, illustrates the precariousness of this position:

> The science to which I pinned my faith is bankrupt. I believed it once. In its name I helped destroy the faith of millions of worshippers in the temples of a thousand creeds. And now they look at me and witness the tragedy of an atheist who has lost his faith. (From *Too True to be Good*, Constable and Co.)

It is powerless

When was the last time you heard someone say, 'Becoming an atheist has turned my life around completely. Before I was an atheist I used to be an alcoholic who beat my wife; now I've become the ideal family man'? Atheism just doesn't have that kind of moral power. The Christian, on the other hand, can point to dozens of examples of the difference that knowing God has made to people's lives.

Charles Bradlaugh, an outstanding intellectual of the nineteenth century, challenged a local preacher of the gospel to a debate in London. The debate was to compare the claims of Christianity with the claims of atheism. The minister, Hugh Price Hughes, agreed to the challenge on one condition: Bradlaugh would bring with him a hundred people whose lives had been changed by their commitment to atheism. If he did so, then Hughes would bring a hundred people whose lives had been changed by knowing God. To drive his point home, Hughes offered to debate with Bradlaugh if he could bring fifty people, or twenty, or ten, and finally if he could bring *one* man or woman whose life had been transformed by atheism. Charles Bradlaugh had to withdraw from the debate. Atheism has no moral power to change lives.

Agnosticism

An agnostic is someone who says that they don't know whether there is a God or not. Perhaps there is, perhaps there isn't. People often spend quite a long time in this state of 'not knowing' as they struggle to find out about God. Anyone who is genuinely unsure must have our respect.

But sometimes people are agnostic in a more aggressive sense: 'Nobody can be certain about anything, so I'm just not going to commit myself either way'. This is the position of the permanent agnostic! But however sensible their stance may seem on the surface, problems appear when we probe a little deeper.

Let's look at the situation logically. Either there is a God or there isn't. One or the other. To the question 'Are you married?' the answers 'Yes' or 'No' are the only two options. 'Possibly' is a nonsense answer! The atheist could be right; those who believe in God could be right. The agnostic is bound to be wrong!

Some consider their agnosticism to be intellectually superior to simple Christianity, as if by sitting on the fence they can enjoy the best of both worlds. But being a fence-sitter can be fatal! Imagine for a moment that you are drowning at sea and two boats arrive to rescue you. They come just as you are going down for the third time. You know that one of the boats has a bomb on it and will explode within minutes, but you don't know which. Because you know only one of the boats can be trusted, you choose to stay in the 'safety' of the water. Sure enough, one of the boats blows up and sinks like a stone, and the other sails off to the safety of a harbour. *You* drown!

You were so right about only one boat being safe, but so wrong about your decision to stay in the water. Dead wrong! This option was 100 per cent doomed to failure. At least on one of the boats you had a 50/50 chance of success. An agnostic is in the same position. Permanently ignoring the only two options, he is condemned to making the wrong choice. Far from being a superior position to hold, it turns out to be the worst of all possible worlds.

And there is more. Many people today reach out for a power beyond themselves. How many of us have half-breathed a prayer to God in the middle of a crisis? The atheist will tell you not to waste your breath – the heavens are empty. Grit your teeth and get on with life. The Christian will say that help is available from a loving God. The agnostic can offer nothing but confusion and doubt!

It's as if you are taking a desperately ill friend to hospital in a strange town. 'Where's the hospital?' you ask anxiously of passers-by. If someone tells you there isn't one, you are upset but resigned to the fact that there's nothing more you can do. If someone tells you there is a hospital and where it is, you race there thankfully to get help for your friend. If someone tells you there may well be a hospital, but they've never heard of it nor do they know where it is if there is one – this is maddeningly frustrating! A glimmer of hope but no way to reach it. 'Thanks for nothing,' you think.

We are beginning to see that this 'not knowing' isn't half as clever as it's made out to be. As a point on the road to discovery it's perfectly sensible; as a settled opinion it's wrong, dangerous and no help to anyone. Agnosticism is like the Dartford Tunnel – all right to travel through, but a nightmare to live in!

God's fingerprints

No one can prove the existence of God, but in a way that's not surprising. Absolutely conclusive proof about anything is very difficult to find. I am sure my wife loves me. I am sure of this because she says so, does loving things and never gives me reason to doubt her. I don't, however, have any concrete proof that she loves me. It is possible that she is just a superb actress and is patiently waiting for the best opportunity to smother me in my sleep and claim the insurance!

What follows is not so much proof as a series of indications that God exists, pointers in his direction. Imagine a thief has broken into and burgled your home, but has been clumsy enough to leave his gloves off. When you arrive home things may appear to be in disarray, but a closer examination reveals fingerprints and clues to the thief's identity. All over our world God has left his fingerprints – divine clues to his existence and identity.

Clue 1 – The exploding supermarket

The first clue in the search to discover whether God exists is found in the remarkable order and design in the universe. Things seem to fit together in an amazing way. If the earth were smaller or larger than it is, it would be unable to sustain an atmosphere we could breathe. If it were a jot nearer the sun, we would fry; a whisker further away and we would freeze. If the earth spun more slowly, if it were tilted at a different angle, if the moon were nearer, if the ozone layer that surrounds the earth were too thin – any one of these things would spell disaster for our planet. Yet – despite our best efforts to destroy the balance of nature by our selfish energy-depleting and environmentally-unfriendly lifestyles – each one of them stays in harmony with the others to enable life on earth to continue.

What about human life itself? Plants produce oxygen which we need; we produce carbon dioxide which plants need. Now there's a clever arrangement! Every cell in the human body has the same number of chromosomes – apart from those which join together to form a new human being; these have exactly half that number so, when they join with a similar cell from someone else, they have the right number again. From this single cell, fingers, legs, hair, skin, blood are formed, not to mention all the intricate workings of the brain, heart and other organs!

Our lives and our universe seem to have a unique designer label – God. What else accounts for such precision handiwork? Chance? Fate? Surely not. This is as hard to believe as an explosion in a supermarket accidentally producing a Christmas roast turkey dinner with all the trimmings!

Isaac Newton, eminent seventeenth-century English physicist and mathematician, once built a model of the solar system to help him in his studies. One day a friend, a fellow scientist and an atheist, came to see him and asked who had made the model. 'Nobody!' Newton replied. When his friend accused him of being ridiculous, Newton asked why, if he could accept that a model needed a maker, did he have such a problem when confronted with the real universe? We all take for granted that the many objects we see around us have designers or builders. However, we also seem quite happy to believe that the most amazing of these – the world and life itself – just happened. This does seem incredibly inconsistent. Isn't it more reasonable to assume that all this order and design in our universe happened because there is a great designer?

Clue 2 – A hole in the middle

The second clue is found in ourselves and our desires and needs. We all have basic drives and instincts which need to be fulfilled. We get hungry, thirsty and cold from time to time and, when we do, we try to meet those needs. A burger takeaway for hunger . . . a Pepsi for thirst . . . and thermal underwear on a cold morning! All these basic desires have a corresponding fulfilment. Just imagine how awful life would be if there was no way for these inner needs to be met: if we had to spend our entire life feeling cold; if we felt desperately tired but there was no such thing as sleep . . . It begins to sound like hell itself! All these deep inner needs have their corresponding fulfilment beyond ourselves: food meets the need called 'hunger', drink meets the need called 'thirst', and so on.

What meets the basic need of human beings to worship? It's hard to find a race of people who don't have this desire in some form or other. Search as we may among even the most remote people groups, we keep coming across belief in some kind of God or gods, some force greater than ourselves and worthy of our worship. And what about the 'civilised' world? Do we think we know better than those less well educated than us and consequently don't feel the need to worship or acknowledge anything greater than ourselves? The evidence suggests otherwise. In Japan – one of the most technologically advanced societies in the world – the Aum Supreme Truth cult, responsible for the nerve gas attack on the Tokyo Underground in 1995, had thousands of members. All kinds of mystical beliefs thrive in places like California, with celebrities like Shirley MacLaine leading the way. Rock star Tina Turner has admitted to being a 'Buddhist Baptist', and actor Richard Gere to being a Buddhist. It's not unusual for all kinds of people in the public eye to talk of their faith, either in mainstream religions or in individual tailor-made belief systems. So much for sophisticated people not having a need to worship something!

This need is found in every continent and in every country, among millions of ordinary, educated people – acknowledged by all the world's major religions and new religious movements. And this is true *despite* opposition to religion: Communists ban it, atheists reject it, dictators abuse it, intellectuals scoff at it and governments suppress it. Yet here we are in the twenty-first century, and religious life of all kinds continues to flourish on our planet! There is a basic human desire for worship of some kind or other.

Now, if each of the needs we mentioned earlier – hunger, thirst, etc – has a corresponding fulfilment, doesn't it seem reasonable that the need to worship would also have one? In other words, is there a God who meets the need for worship? If there is no God, this need is the only one of all our needs to which there is no solution.

Let's think about our own lives, and the lives of those we know. It's very common to experience, from time to time, at least a fleeting feeling that there must be more to life than what appears on the surface: a half-curse, half-prayer shouted at God in a crisis; the thought of being reunited with someone you love as you stand by a graveside. All these are indications that deep within us we cry out for something greater than ourselves. Blaise Pascal, seventeenth-century French philosopher and mathematician, said that inside every person is a God-shaped vacuum, a sort of hole in the middle of our beings. We have, he said, a need that only God can meet. All the indications are that he was right!

Clue 3 – Mugging rules OK?

The fact that we know right from wrong points to the existence of God. Most human beings have a remarkable amount in common in this area. We agree that killing someone is wrong. We have no hesitation in condemning dishonesty, greed and selfishness, along with rape and mugging. We may even do some of these things ourselves, but we know that moral and ethical boundaries exist and certainly expect others to abide by them! Even our daily conversation betrays our belief in values or standards to which we ought to conform:

- 'I ought to visit my elderly mother.'
- 'How could they do that to a child?'
- 'It's disgusting what young people get up to these days!'

But where do these values come from? If the atheist is right, why should we care what we do? If there is no God, then we have no supreme power to whom we are accountable and anything goes! Yet it's almost impossible to imagine the kind of society in which betraying your friends, sexually assaulting your children or mugging pensioners is accepted as perfectly reasonable.

So where *do* these standards come from? Some people have

argued that each society decides what is right for itself. However, a close look at the histories of some of the world's great societies shows remarkable unanimity between them. The ancient Egyptian, Roman, Greek and Chinese cultures have major areas of agreement with our own. Far from each culture setting their own unique standards, they all appear to have conformed to an objective standard beyond themselves.

For centuries people have tried to come up with alternatives to God as the source of all moral boundaries, but none of these suggestions comes close to explaining why we know right from wrong in the first place. What is incredible is that some in our society write God off – yet still maintain their value system. If we are all here by accident, subject to the vagaries of chance throughout our lives, only to die with no hope of a future, who cares about standards and values? If we are just advanced animals, let's behave like animals! Yet no society actually lives like this.

Our values must have come from somewhere. It's at least reasonable to believe they came from a moral, wise mind. Christians call this mind *God*.

Clue 4 – A cosmic lottery

What is the purpose of life? Why are we here? What does it all mean? If there is no God, the human race just happened, evolving by chance from the primeval slime. We are a random collection of atoms flung together over millions of years, finally emerging as the human race. A huge accident. Numbers spat out at random by a giant, inter-galactic ball machine in a cosmic version of the National Lottery – the whole of our lives, our very existence adding up to one big fluke.

Serious atheists down the centuries have expressed this meaninglessness which, they have to agree, is the logical conclusion of their atheism. Hear the utter hopelessness in the words of eighteenth-century philosopher, Baron de Montesquieu:

> We should weep for men at their birth, not at their death.

Why? Because life is meaningless and we should pity those who have to go through it. Feel the futility and uselessness that permeates this observation by American writer Mark Twain near the end of his life:

> Men are born, they labour and sweat and struggle; they squabble and scold and fight; those they love are taken from them, and the joy of life is turned to aching grief. The release comes at last and they vanish from a world where they were of no consequence . . . a world which will lament them a day and forget them forever.

And twentieth-century philosopher Albert Camus:

> What is intolerable is to see one's life drained of meaning. To be told that there is no reason for existing. A man can't live without some reason for living.

And Jean-Paul Sartre:

> This world is not the product of intelligence. It meets our gaze as would a crumpled piece of paper . . . What is man but a little puddle of water whose freedom is death?

In 1889 philosopher Friedrich Nietzsche suffered a permanent nervous breakdown and spent the last ten years of his life in a lunatic asylum – partly, according to his biographer, the result of trying to live with the logic of his position as an atheist.

All these men saw that the end result of their atheism was that life became absurd and meaningless. However, thousands of atheists don't want to face this fact because it is too painful, and thousands of others live in ignorance of their true position. It's as if a fish denied the existence of water while continuing to swim in it and to feed on other life growing there. Many atheists want to reject God but hold on to what belief in God provides – meaning and purpose! They may live their entire lives without being aware of the depressing consequences of atheism. If they were aware of it, the sense of desolation would be overwhelming.

Human life cries out for fulfilment. Belief in God offers us a possible explanation for our existence, security from knowing that our future has a destiny, and therefore a reason for living. Atheism is a broken, empty philosophy in comparison.

Clue 5 – Whodunnit?

Sometimes my wife Janet and I have disagreements. Something has been left on the living-room floor – a mug of half-drunk tea, a newspaper or a set of keys. There now follows a dramatic dialogue:

> *Janet (tidying up) speaks first*
> – Who put that there?
> – Don't look at me!
> – I *am* looking at you.
> – I didn't put it there!
> – Who else could have?
> – Perhaps *you* did!
> – Don't be ridiculous!

The point that our minor domestic tiff illustrates is this: despite the disagreement, there is one thing on which we are absolutely united – *somebody* left it there. Whodunnit? Somebody did. It didn't appear by magic. If Janet and I didn't agree on this simple fact, we would have no basis on which to argue. The principle we are operating on is this: everything is caused by something. The paper this book is written on came from a tree which came from a seed which came from a tree . . . and so on. I came into being through my parents, and they, would you believe, came into being through *their* parents. Nothing in our lives just 'happened' or started without something making it happen.

We are forced to ask what it was that started the whole thing off in the very beginning. You might say it was chance or fate, but this doesn't really help us. Chance or luck is not the *cause* of anything, just a description of events for which we can't find an adequate cause or reason. For example, if a 200-to-1-against horse with a limp and one eye wins the Grand National, we describe that as lucky or a fluke. But this 'chance' element didn't *cause* the horse to win. It merely describes the fact that we can't explain how it won. So to say that the universe started by chance is just like saying that it started but we don't know how.

This brings us to the other alternative: God started it. This is a reasonable possibility and stands up well to the other options. 'This world is here because someone put it here' is a statement to be taken very seriously.

Clue 6 – Pleased to meet you

Thousands and thousands of people claim to have met him – God, that is. They say he has changed their lives. Without giving it more than a few seconds' thought I can think of doctors, bricklayers, lawyers, housewives, secretaries, teachers and care-takers who could all talk about meeting God. There are retired people, children and every age in between. People from Asia, Africa and America. Black people and white people. And these are just some of those known to me personally! It's very difficult to write them all off as cranks, unintelligent or gullible. What is it that has changed their lives? A belief that there really is a God who can be encountered and who changes lives.

Atheism and agnosticism are no longer the great 'bogeymen' to belief in God they once were. Today the humanist, material-ist worldview, in which both atheism and agnosticism have their roots, is seen to have flaws and not be quite the engine to progress we once thought. The sense of futility this worldview has generated has led many to question its effects. In spite of our science-based, technological culture, we still have a deep longing for mystical, spiritual and emotional experiences. This means that people are no longer so rejecting of the spiritual as they once were, and more open to the possibility of God's existence.

Unfortunately, the failure of humanistic materialism has also raised doubt that *any* worldview can claim to know the absolute truth or give an all-embracing explanation about life, the uni-verse and everything. The reasoning goes like this: what I am experiencing may not be the same as your experience, so it wouldn't be right or proper for me to make any judgements about your situation or to impose my solutions. This attitude permeates right through to religious belief – the general feeling is that no religion has 'cornered the market' on truth or is relevant for everyone everywhere.

So, although it is more likely in today's world than in previous generations that a person *will* believe in God – it may not necessarily be God as understood by Christians. Recent years have seen a rise in 'irrational' belief systems – New Age philosophy, paganism and interest in the occult, for example – and a 'mix and match' approach to religion abounds which mirrors our consumerist culture. As it becomes more difficult for churches to assume that everyone shares the Christian worldview, or even knows what that worldview is, one of the main means of 'proving' God's existence will be by individual Christians revealing his presence in their lives.

If you can say that *you are certain* there is no God, then you won't want to go any further with this book. If you *are* willing to admit the possibility of God's existence but still have more questions, read on!

2

What about all the suffering?

On Wednesday morning 13th March 1996 ... Thomas Hamilton burst into the gym at Dunblane Primary School. Three minutes later a teacher and sixteen small bodies lay scattered like rag dolls around the hall – dead or dying. Amongst the sea of floral tributes and soft toys that spread for over half a mile along the Doune road lies a solitary bunch of flowers. Its card carried no poetry nor sentimental message. There is just one, stark three-letter word, WHY? (From the text of the message preached on the Sunday evening following Dunblane, at the Church of God, Parkburn Road, Kilsyth, by the senior minister John Glass, and printed in *Direction* magazine, May 1996, p12.)

It would take a cold, hard person not to share the heartache of the people of Dunblane after this tragic event. Many of us have asked similar questions. Why did my mother die of cancer? Why was my best friend paralysed in a car accident? Why are so many people starving to death?

The question of suffering boils down to this: how can a God of love let all this suffering go on in his world? Either he doesn't exist at all, or he is a vicious tyrant who enjoys seeing people in pain! This seems to present a pretty strong case against the existence of a loving God, and there certainly is no slick or easy answer to the problem of suffering. But perhaps the answer is more like a jigsaw puzzle, with large pieces that fit together to make a picture. Our confusion at this massive puzzle (how can a loving, powerful God stand by while we suffer?) becomes clearer if we take it one piece at a time.

Jigsaw piece 1

The hard truth is that we have only *ourselves* to blame for much of the suffering in our world. It's no good blaming God when a drunken driver kills an innocent pedestrian, or when a football hooligan knifes one of your friends on the way home from the match. Both these incidents, and others like them, point the finger at the real culprits – the human race. God can hardly be blamed for suffering we choose to bring on ourselves. Bloodshed in Bosnia, mass murder in Rwanda, thousands crushed to death in the Twin Towers terrorist attack of September 11, 2001 – such terrible atrocities replicated around the word reveal the horrifying consequences of man's inhumanity to man. When nations hoard food and refuse aid to the hungry, when governments declare war on each other, when gangs terrorise housing estates, when adults sexually abuse children, when old people are robbed and beaten, *we* are to blame.

Now it is true that we *personally* may not be to blame for *all* these problems, but we *are* personally to blame for *some* things. No one reading this book can honestly say they have never caused anyone *any* suffering. Never an angry word to your partner or child? Never a selfish action at work? Never a refusal to help someone in need? No, the plain fact is that, to a greater or lesser degree, we *all* contribute to the suffering in the world.

This was illustrated a century ago by the response to a competition in a national newspaper. Readers were asked to write on the theme 'What's wrong with the world?' From thousands of entries the winner was a man whose letter was the briefest:

> Dear Sir,
> I am,
> Yours faithfully . . .

God could only get rid of the suffering we inflict on ourselves by getting rid of *us* (pretty drastic!) or by turning us into androids who only acted on his command. Both these options would rob us of freedom of choice. We have been given the privilege of free will, so we have to live with the consequences of exercising that freedom. Both suffering and joy come from having choice.

Some argue that there is a further option. Why can't God *stop* the actions of bad people? The bullet from a killer's gun could metamorphose into a feather; a mugger's knife could turn into a banana as it was raised to strike . . .

But to do this God would have to intervene in our affairs all the time and be continually throwing the laws of nature into chaos. Without consistent laws we would never know where we were; life would be a nightmare of confusion and unpredictability.

Compare it to playing tennis with a friend. If he persistently double faults, you may, to be kind, give him another chance to serve. If he trips, you may agree to play the point again. But if you both ignore the rules, the lines and the net completely, you are simply not playing tennis. It has become a different game altogether, or no kind of game at all. So it is with God in our world. He can intervene from time to time, but basically he has to uphold the laws of the 'game'. Without these dependable rules we could not exist. This means, sadly, that whether a knife is stuck into wood or human flesh, damage is the consequence.

Jigsaw piece 2

What about the suffering we *don't* cause, the things we have no control over – like earthquakes, famine, volcanoes and other natural disasters? Strange as it may seem, even here we must take some responsibility.

Earthquakes have indeed caused death, homelessness and injury on a huge scale. Thousands suffered in major quakes in Mexico in 1985 and in Japan in 1995, for example. What is not as well known is that a vast amount of suffering could have been prevented. As long ago as 1906 earthquakes were monitored and the resulting devastation scrutinised. After the San Francisco earthquake at that time, Dr T Nakamura was sent by the Japanese government to the earthquake zone to assess why there had been such colossal loss of life, injury and devastation. In his report this sentence stands out: 'Dishonest mortar was responsible for nearly all the earthquake damage.' In other words, the damage could have been drastically reduced by decent, reinforced buildings!

Twenty-nine years later, in 1935, we read this report in *The Times* after a major earthquake in Pakistan:

> The appalling destruction in Quetta City is traced to the poor constructional quality of the buildings. Such earthquake-proof build-

ings as had been built in the area survived the catastrophe. Not even their chimneys fell.

What is absolutely staggering is that, after the Mexican earthquake on 8 October 1985, the same newspaper, *The Times*, wrote that among the reasons for the disaster were . . .

> . . . second-rate workmanship and skimping on construction materials. There is wide agreement that many buildings need not have fallen, and that many lives could have been saved had some builders been more scrupulous. Probably the strongest lesson from the Mexico City disaster is that good architecture works.

For over 90 years we have known how to minimise earthquake damage, but disasters like Mexico reveal how little we put this knowledge into practice.

There are human dimensions to other natural disasters, too. For example, thousands suffered and died in the last century from famine in Africa; but years before it happened, relief organisations were warning governments that famine was coming. All too often corrupt rulers spend millions on lavish premises or military equipment while their people starve. A great deal of pain and suffering could be avoided if governments and individuals acted differently.

It does seem unreasonable to blame God for our own unwillingness as human beings to act responsibly. Disaster after disaster in our world entails human failure either causing the catastrophe or making it considerably worse. We *do* have to carry the can for this ourselves. But, having said all that, there is suffering which appears to be beyond our control – natural disasters that strike without warning and seemingly without cause. How can we explain these?

Christians believe that God made a perfect world. Unfortunately, people decided they knew better than God how things ought to be run, and turned their backs on him. This resulted in a rift between God and the human race which, like the fallout after a nuclear accident, also had an effect on creation. A once-perfect world became imperfect, and human beings found themselves in alien, hostile territory, surrounded by a natural environment 'red in tooth and claw', infected by sickness and disease. (You can read the full story in the first three chapters of the Bible.) So we are at the mercy of disasters which are symptoms of the malfunction in the relationship between ourselves and our Creator.

Jigsaw piece 3

This is quite a small piece of the jigsaw really, but it is the one we feel most – pain. We tend to take this aspect of suffering very personally! If we, or people we love, endure long periods of pain, we tend to get angry with God for letting the suffering go on.

But it would be disastrous if God were to remove pain completely. Without pain my appendix could burst with no warning; my teeth could go rotten and I would never know; I could lose whole limbs in a fire without realising it. When I go to the doctor, he asks me where the pain is – this helps him to locate the problem and attempt a diagnosis and cure. Without pain, his job would be much more difficult! Pain, far from being an enemy, can be our friend. It is the body's early-warning system. Without it, life would be unimaginably worse than it is now.

Dr Paul Brand, a leading specialist in the study of pain, researched for years into the reasons for pain, particularly in connection with leprosy. He recounts incident after tragic incident of patients who lost all sensation of pain in one or more limbs – hands cut to the bone during routine domestic jobs, fingers bitten right off, toes severed while a patient was digging a garden – all without any realisation of what was happening. No wonder Dr Brand says, 'Thank God for inventing pain. I don't think he could have done a better job.'

Perhaps we should pause for a moment to see how far we have come in piecing together the great jigsaw puzzle of suffering. We have admitted that the human race brings a great deal of trouble on itself and could do a great deal more to alleviate suffering. As long as we have freedom of choice, some of us will choose to cause suffering. We have seen that we live in an imperfect natural world which is potentially hostile to us. And we have noted that pain is not the great enemy it often appears to be.

Now we must be absolutely honest and say that all this still leaves us with large gaps in our jigsaw. None of the points we have discussed so far provides a complete explanation when we are faced with a badly deformed baby, a major aeroplane disaster or a horribly disfigured accident victim. No one, anywhere in the world, has a totally convincing answer to the problem of suffering. But Christians have two more pieces of the jigsaw to help us come to terms with it.

Jigsaw piece 4

God understands our suffering because he himself has experienced it! No one can accuse God of being an uninvolved deity, just sitting back and watching us suffer. He sent his Son to earth to check it out for himself, to experience firsthand what life was all about for the human race. The following story, called 'The Long Silence', gives a powerful portrayal of God's action:

> At the end of time, billions of people were scattered on a great plain before God's throne. Most shrank back from the brilliant light before them. But some groups near the front talked heatedly, not with cringing shame but with belligerence.
>
> 'Can God judge us? What does he know about suffering?' snapped a woman with dark hair. Her body showed the tell-tale ravages of the torture chamber. 'I've endured terror . . . beating . . . rape . . . death!'
>
> In another group, a young African opened his shirt. 'What about this?' he demanded, revealing bullet holes. 'Killed for no crime but belonging to the wrong tribe!'
>
> In another crowd, a young man with sullen eyes: 'I've got AIDS,' he murmured. 'Why me? Why should I suffer?'
>
> Far out across the plain were hundreds of such groups. Each had a complaint against God for the evil and suffering he had permitted

in his world. 'How lucky God is to live in heaven where everything is sweetness and light, where there is no weeping or fear, no hunger or hatred. What does God know of all that the human race has been forced to endure? For God leads a pretty sheltered life,' they said.

So each of these groups sent out a leader, chosen because he or she had suffered most – someone who had endured terrible pain, someone who had been killed by a bomb, a murder victim, a horribly deformed arthritic, someone born with brain damage, an abused child . . . In the centre of the plain these leaders consulted with each other. At last they were ready to present their case. It was rather clever.

Before God could be qualified to be their judge, he must endure what they endured. They decided that God should be sentenced to live on earth – as a man! Let him be born a Jew. Let people think him illegitimate. Let him live in a country occupied and ruled by a cruel, callous government. Give him a work so difficult that even his family would think him out of his mind when he tried to do it. Let him be betrayed by his closest friends. Let him face false charges, be tried by a prejudiced jury and convicted by a cowardly judge. Let him be beaten and tortured. At the last, let him see what it means to be terribly alone. Then let him die. Let him die so that there can be no doubt that he died. Let there be a host of witnesses to his death.

As each leader announced his or her portion of the sentence, loud murmurs of approval went up from the throng of people assembled. When the last person had finished pronouncing sentence, there was a long silence. No one uttered another word. No one moved. For suddenly all knew that God had already served his sentence.

Many people find great comfort from the knowledge that God has endured human suffering and understands what we go through. He has been where we are – the chief executive has experience of life on the shop floor, the captain has worked in the engine room, the chief of police has walked the beat. God has been down here at the sharp end.

For whatever reason God chose to make man as he is – limited and suffering and subject to sorrows and death. He had the honesty and the courage to take His own medicine. Whatever game He is playing with His creation He has kept His own rules and played fair. He has Himself gone through the whole of human experience, from the trivial irritations of family life and lack of money to the worst horrors, pain, humiliation, defeat, despair and death. He was born in poverty and died in disgrace and felt it well worthwhile. (From *The Man Born to be King* by Dorothy Sayers, Gollancz, an imprint of Cassell plc, 1947.)

Jigsaw piece 5

The best treatment for a bleeding wound is a bandage, not a lecture on suffering! When we are suffering, most of us want not clever answers to philosophical questions but practical, down-to-earth help. If we deny the existence of a loving God (by saying he is a figment of our imagination or he exists but won't come to our rescue) we rob ourselves of the major source of relief. If there is no God, everything that happens is a result of chance. Not much comfort there! If he just doesn't care, that's even worse! What a terrible position to be in.

In contrast, Christians believe in a God who can help. Despite many misunderstandings, Christianity is not pie-in-the-sky-when-you-die; it's more like life-right-here-on-the-ground-while-you're-still-around! It's about a relationship with someone who is with us in every difficulty and who promises never to leave us however tough it gets.

In fact, the kind of help God provides isn't easy to beat! And with it comes a guarantee to every Christian that all unanswered questions will one day have answers, all wrongs be put to right, and life will be enjoyed forever without suffering of any kind. This promise has strengthened and encouraged Christians over the centuries. It sounds a fantastic offer, and it is. Be careful not to reject it too quickly. If you dismiss it without thought, what an idiot you would feel one second after you die to discover it was true!

What it adds up to is this. There is a tremendous amount of pain in individual lives. We have been promised help and support in this life and a complete absence of suffering in the next. There is not much else on offer, so we might as well check out what there is pretty carefully.

Many thinkers have proffered their own tentative explanations as to why suffering is allowed in our world. For C S Lewis, 'God whispers to us in our pleasures, speaks in our conscience, but shouts in our pain: it is his megaphone to rouse a deaf world'. So suffering is used by God to act as a global conscience, focusing our attention on life's vital issues. Alexander Solzhenitsyn's own experience of suffering taught him many things about himself, and he came to be grateful for it: 'It was only when I lay there on rotting prison straw that I sensed within myself the first stirrings of good. So, bless you, prison, for having been in my life'.

Wherever we are, bad experiences can teach us many things and we may even admit that we would have been worse as people without them. However, even with all the pieces in this chapter, the jigsaw is still incomplete. Although Christians have some extra pieces, honesty compels us to say that we have not got to the bottom of the problem of suffering. To some extent we are all in a fog on this issue, blindly groping our way towards the answer. The major difference is that Christians can see a dim light in the distance drawing them on; others must struggle on towards an ever-deepening blackness.

3

What about other religions?

Fifty or a hundred years ago, few people in the Western world would have thought this a very important question. Now we are all aware of the many faiths which vie for our attention. Accessible plane flights have faciliated speedy travel all over the planet. The Sikh family we used to read about in our school textbooks now lives next door. Television exposes us to the range of world religions. Suddenly our cosy little world is shattered by the insight that not everyone thinks, believes or acts like we do.

In the year 2000 there were over 1.1 billion Muslims in the world and 0.8 billion Hindus, compared with 2 billion Christians. For the past 30 years Muslims and Hindus have grown at a faster rate than Christians, at 2.6% and 1.9% respectively per year, compared with 1.6% for Christians. When you add in the followers of Confucius, the adherents to Buddhism, and all other non-Christian religions, you will see that two-thirds of the world's population are not Christians. In the UK in 2000 there were 675,000 active Muslims meeting in 660 registered mosques, and 400,000 active Hindus meeting in 225 temples.

Hardly surprising then, that you will hear the argument: 'Surely Christianity isn't saying that the majority of people in the world have got it wrong? Isn't it arrogant to believe that Christians are the only ones who have got it right?'

Is sincerity enough?

In conversation with people who are not committed Christians I have been told, 'I think genuine followers of all religions will get there in the end; God wouldn't reject anyone who was sincere.'

On the surface this seems a perfectly reasonable statement, and a very attractive one too because it credits God with generosity and ourselves with tolerance. It also means there is no need to work hard to examine the evidence and discover the truth. People can believe what they want as long as they are sincere.

Despite this, I am afraid that we have to reject the sincerity option for two reasons.

It's wrong

Sincerity is not enough. Adolf Hitler may have been completely sincere in his desire to eliminate the Jews and create a super race. But very few people would say that the slaughter of six million Jews was right! The best we can say for Hitler is that he was sincerely wrong.

What about you and me? We may sincerely believe that Dallas is in Africa, that the moon is made of cheese or that a Mars bar is a pub on another planet! But we would be wrong. Nobody is going to be impressed if, having heard all the scientific evidence to the contrary, we persist in saying 'But I *sincerely* believe the moon is made of cheese!' What if millions sincerely believed that the earth was flat? People did once, and they were wrong! Sincerity doesn't make wrong facts right.

However hard you think, it's impossible to come up with an everyday example which supports the theory that all you need is sincerity. We just don't live like that; it wouldn't work.

It's dangerous

Imagine you have a very young child who suddenly comes out in a rash. A friend who happens to be visiting you says there's nothing to worry about – her daughter had the same rash when she was a baby. 'It goes away in a couple of weeks,' you are assured. Ten days later your child is rushed into hospital, his life only just saved by the intervention of a skilled medical team. What went wrong? A well-meaning friend misled you. The rash looked the same, but it wasn't. Her sincerity is not in question – she genuinely wanted to help; but her advice turned out to be wrong. This kind of sincerity can be fatal! What you and your young child needed most was not a sincere diagnosis but an *accurate* one!

All this is even more crucial in matters of religious belief. Christians maintain that our personal destiny is at stake; get the facts wrong and we could miss out on real fulfilment now and life with God for ever when we die. What we need desperately is not a sincere view of God but an *accurate* one. There is nothing more tragic than committing yourself to a system of beliefs or a lifestyle which is ultimately futile. It would be like spending a lifetime climbing a ladder, only to discover at the top that the ladder is leaning against the wrong wall!

So we are forced to conclude that even if you are the most sincere person in the world, you could still be wrong. To be sincere is not enough.

Before we examine the claim that Christianity is unique, let's try to clear up two popular misunderstandings. Both seem extremely plausible, but in reality are like the house fronts on a Hollywood film set – when you look behind them there's nothing there!

Misunderstanding 1: 'All roads lead to God'

This view holds that, whatever faith or religious outlook you have, everyone ends up at the same place. Different religions are just different routes to the same destination, so it doesn't really matter which one you believe.

Does this argument hold water? Are people really saying that all religious beliefs, from every culture in the world, from all the years of history and all the new religious movements in the future, are all leading to God? How can this be when so many different things are believed, many of which are the exact opposite of somebody else's belief? For example, some people believe that God is pleased by animal sacrifices, while others believe that God is appalled by them. They cannot be worshipping the same God!

Such is the variety of religious belief, you might as well say it doesn't matter what you believe as long as you are sincere! No, I'm afraid this option just doesn't add up.

We might say that only the *major* world religions lead to God? But how can we determine which religions are major? Which should be left out? What criteria shall we use to decide? Even if we take the five most commonly thought of as the world's major religions, a brief examination reveals mammoth differences between them. Hinduism believes in many gods; Islam is absolutely insistent there is only one. Buddhism is silent about the nature of God or even whether he exists; Judaism describes his character in detail. Christians believe that in this world there is only one life and one death for each individual; Buddhists believe that we keep returning to this world in a series of multiple reincarnations.

What about the way of salvation, the way to eternal life? Many ancient religions offer salvation through gifts and offerings to the gods, even human sacrifices. In Hinduism we discover that fulfilment of duty, ceremonial observance and discipline lead to salvation. Muslims must fulfil their obligations to fast and pray, and recite their creed; only then, though they may taste judgement, can they enter paradise. Christians, in opposition to all the others, say salvation can't be earned by doing anything; you receive it as a gift.

So we can see that the world's major religions are not going in the same direction or to the same destination. It's only possible to believe that 'all roads lead to God' if we remain ignorant about these different religions (the roads) and their view of God (the destination). All religions do not lead to the same point any more than all aeroplanes from Heathrow go to New York or all roads from Luton lead to London!

People who believe that all the world's religions somehow happily combine are likely to have a very hazy, sentimental view of the way they do fit together. They may imagine that God is something like a huge painting. Each religion completes one part of the picture, each of them true but just not the whole story, with God (the painting) big enough to contain all their views and ideas.

The reality is that the world's religions are not just different but *contradictory*. Taking the idea of God being a painting, some religions would be happy with the one painting idea, while others would say there are several paintings, all different, and yet others would argue that the painting is irrelevant and therefore the frame is probably empty! *Somebody is wrong*. To say 'All roads lead to God' is as illogical as saying that a bus ride to the local shops is much the same as a trip to the moon in a spaceship. The route, mode of transport and destination are all completely different!

Misunderstanding 2: 'I'm sure it helps *you*'

Probably never before has there been so much choice in life. In almost every sphere of our lives, the number and variety of options are immense. Sales techniques major on the fact that Product X may be alright for others, but Product Y is what you and your family really need. Try asking for a painkiller from your chemist. Aspirin or paracetamol? Tablet or capsule or liquid? Brand name or chemist's own? Regular or extra strength? Small or large packet? It's enough to *give* you a headache!

In Western culture, the 'customer is king' mentality has infiltrated even the area of belief. We accept new religions with all the indifference with which we greet a new supermarket or restaurant chain. 'He is a Hindu and I am a Christian' is seen as little more than an accident of birth, taste and culture. 'He has chosen Hinduism; that's fine for him. I have chosen Christianity and that suits me'; as if the choice is as insignificant as saying 'He eats at McDonalds; that's fine for him. I eat at Burger King and that suits me.'

Now it's true that in the religious 'supermarket' we do have a choice. The difference is that this choice has far-reaching implications. These products are very different and their effect on our lives is total. A belief is either true for everybody or nobody. Christianity is more like gravity than stamp-collecting, a fact rather than an option. There is no middle ground: either Christianity is true – whether or not we believe it – or it isn't. To say that it's all right for someone else but not for you is both patronising and wrong. The Christian faith claims to open the way to God and to answer profound questions about life and death. These answers are either right (for everybody) or wrong (for everybody).

Christianity claims to be unique

There is little doubt about what Christianity claims for itself. Here are two quotations from the Bible, the Christian's manual of faith:

I am the way, the truth and the life! Without me, no one can go to the Father.

(The words of Jesus recorded in John 14:6)

Only Jesus has the power to save! His name is the only one in all the world that can save anyone.

(Peter speaking about Jesus in Acts 4:12)

Both these verses indicate the claim to exclusiveness of Christianity. Faith in Jesus is seen as the *only way* to find God. No amount of fudging can remove the clear thrust of statements like these.

At first glance these claims seem harsh and unbending, even incredibly arrogant! But if you think about it, isn't all truth ultimately like this? Two plus two equals four. I may want it to equal five, or seven, or even 77, but the fact is that the answer is four. Five might seem near enough, but actually it has more in common with 77 – both are wrong! In practice we *expect* the truth to be exclusive – excluding what is wrong. Christianity claims to be *the* truth about the way to God; the nature of this claim makes it impossible to reconcile it with other religions. They may contain truth but only Christianity is the whole truth.

In contrast to this, other religions have an inclusiveness which is superficially attractive. Most of them can absorb Jesus and his teachings under their general umbrella. Hinduism, in particular, has room for Jesus among its many gods. But it is this very inclusiveness which should worry a determined seeker after truth. Let's go back to the arithmetic to illustrate this.

$2 + 2 = 4$	5 or 7 or 11 or 2,476,312 etc, etc.
truth	**error**

Notice that, by its very nature, *error is more inclusive than truth*. In this case it is able to include absolutely every number other than four! This tends to suggest that the very inclusiveness which is claimed to be enlightened or tolerant by many religious movements turns out to be just plain error wearing a fancy hat! Christianity's very exclusiveness is an indication that it may be the truth.

Perhaps we ought to pause for a moment to clarify what Christianity is *not* saying. It is not saying that all the teaching in every other religion is completely wrong. Many of the things they teach are morally uplifting and promote high ethical standards. Neither are genuine Christians looking down on other people who have different beliefs, with a dismissive arrogance or superior attitude. The Christian perspective is simply that we have all been faced with an ultimatum from God: 'Come to me on the basis of my Son's death for you. This is the way, take it or leave it.' And Christians are those who have decided to come and are thrilled that they did. Christians did not make Christianity exclusive and cannot change it any more than we can change the law of gravity. They, along with the rest of the human race, are faced with a choice: am I going to accept that this exclusive claim is true? Yes or no. Our destiny will be decided by the answer!

Christianity *is* unique

We have seen that Christianity claims to be unique, but how is this uniqueness seen in practice? Let's consider some of the main differences between being a Christian and following another religion.

Salvation is not earned

All religions other than Christianity have a kind of points system for obtaining eternal life. Hindus must live to the best of their ability and refrain from hurting even the lowliest of animals in order to achieve a better kind of life next time round. If they live bad lives, they may be reincarnated to a more destitute human existence or even come back as another species, such as an insect. Muslims must fulfil a number of obligations if they are to receive salvation: they must abstain from alcohol, make a pilgrimage to Mecca, fast during the month of Ramadan and pray five times a day. Buddhists must strive to overcome desire if they want to obtain salvation. Each religious movement has its own rules to follow if you are to be acceptable to God.

This is where Christianity is completely different. Let's look at that manual again:

> The reward for sin is death. But God's gift is eternal life given by Jesus Christ our Lord.
>
> Romans 6:23

> You were saved by faith in God, who treats us much better than we deserve. This is God's gift to you, and not anything you have done on your own.
>
> Ephesians 2:8,9

The Christian faith says that the points system doesn't work; no one will ever accumulate enough to pass heaven's entrance exam. The kindest, nicest person on the face of the earth still fails to achieve the pass mark – perfection. There is, in fact, a 100 per cent failure rate. So far so bad!

The good news is that Jesus lived a perfect life and became the only person ever to make the grade. God then says to a world of exam failures that, as a graduation present for his Son, he would like to offer us salvation – eternal life in heaven and his presence with us now – as a free gift; not on the basis of what we have earned or what we deserve, but because of what his Son has accomplished. Unlike other religions we can do absolutely nothing to win salvation; we must simply receive it as a free gift.

'But Christianity *does* have rules and regulations like any other faith. What about going to church and loving your neighbour and not committing adultery?'

Yes, it's true that there are rules to follow in Christianity, but they have a totally different rationale behind them. Put briefly, they are a *result* of salvation, not the cause of it. It's a little like my relationship with my wife. I try to show my love for her by helping with our children, doing jobs around the house and buying the occasional bunch of flowers. None of this is to win her love; she already loves me. In fact, a diamond necklace and a BMW would not make her love me if she had not chosen to do so already. In a similar way, no amount of effort on my part will earn God's love; but, because he already loves me, I want to express my gratitude by following his rules.

This makes the Christian faith fundamentally different from other viewpoints. These others follow rules and regulations out of duty and fear of the consequences of disobedience, hoping for salvation in the future. Christians follow rules and regulations out of love and gratitude for a salvation *already received* in the present. A vast difference!

God's search for man

The story of religious movements is the story of man's search for God. People have looked for God in ritual and ceremony, in mystical experiences, in asceticism, in holy places, in religious belief and fervent devotion. They have searched in ancient faiths and in modern cults, in eastern magic and Western materialism, in profound thought and orgies of emotion. The search has been unsuccessful, as unsuccessful as an ant trying to find the planet Jupiter! Man is simply not capable of this feat. Which is why Christianity is the story of the God who searches for man, the God who wants to be known and so introduces himself to us in the person of Jesus. In Christianity, unlike other religions, *God* has taken the initiative. He wants to be found. The details of his whereabouts are in the Bible and this information is available to everyone. God is not playing hard to get!

Real assurance

The Christian faith offers a sense of security. Ask Christians if they are going to be with God for ever and they will answer 'yes!'. Followers of other faiths will invariably say 'possibly' or 'perhaps' – it all depends on whether or not they can keep up their efforts and build up more on the positive side than the negative side when they die. Because salvation for them is gained by earning merit no one can never tell if enough has been earned, no one can be sure they are really going to make it!

It is such a relief to know that God has done everything necessary for our salvation! Our only response is faith. Once we have made this commitment, he takes the waiting out of wanting. Do you want a certain hope for the future now, without having to wait until you're dead to find out for sure whether or not you have made the grade? God offers this certainty *now* to those who receive his Son.

Moral power

In a world where sin makes drowning men of us all, other religions may provoke discussion about the water but Christianity throws us the life-jacket! In other words, we are given practical guidelines that we can put into action whenever we are out of our depth.

And this is not just a code for living, but a power for living. When we become Christians, God's power comes into us and gives us strength to overcome things in our lives that we know are wrong. Power to defeat bad habits, alter our thinking, love the unlovely – a special offer of 'power for good' available only with this product! This transformation can have far-reaching consequences.

I'll give you an example. In the 1960s a young woman's Christian faith took her on a journey to Hong Kong, to begin a ministry to drug addicts in the notorious Walled City. She encountered many difficulties and dangers, but today Jackie Pullinger's ministry has resulted in thousands of addicts being able to escape the stranglehold of their addiction and to live new lives as God's power works in them.

The story of the uniqueness of the Christian faith does not end with its moral power. We could talk about the way Christianity is less culturally bound than other faiths, with Christians in every racial grouping; how it cuts across barriers of age, sex, culture, continent and colour; about its unparalleled record of social concern and care for the underprivileged; about its survival under intense persecution.

Christianity claims to be unique and, under scrutiny, shows itself to be unique. We are faced with a choice – is it right or wrong?

4

What's so great about Jesus?

Remember the Beatles? In the early 1970s they believed they were more popular than Jesus. True, over 30 years on their music is still being played, enjoyed and analysed. But it would be hard to justify a claim that they were more enduringly fascinating than the person of the Son of God. Interest in Jesus hasn't waned, some 2000 years after he lived. Take the film *Jesus*, for example. It's been translated into over 300 languages and seen by hundreds of millions of people – more than any other film ever produced! This level of interest highlights what ordinary people have thought for centuries: this Jesus character is someone special.

But what was Jesus really like? Among the wilder suggestions have been that he was a gay hippy, an alien from outer space or a time-traveller who turns up at various points in history whenever the world needs a little extra help. More seriously, he has been portrayed as a political revolutionary, a great moral teacher, an eastern mystic and a misunderstood miracle-worker. Christians claim that he is not just a wonderful human being, he is also God; that he isn't dead now, although he was for a few days; that he is very interested in making contact with every person on our planet.

Let's try to put aside what we think we know about Jesus and examine the facts.

Did Jesus really exist?

There are still a few people who believe that Jesus was just a figment of someone's imagination. If this is so, it's strange that no one pointed out the fictitious nature of the Gospels when they were first circulated. For one thing, who were the brilliant minds who wove all that deep moral teaching into a sort of first-century novel?

For another, all the manuscript evidence (see next chapter) points to *reporters* at work rather than novelists.

Besides this, how can we explain the impact that Jesus Christ has made on our world if he never existed? Whenever you date a letter or write a cheque, you confirm the existence of Jesus: 1 January 2003, 2004, 2005 and so on – but 2003 or 2004 years since what? Since England won the World Cup? Since the invention of the wheel? Of course not! All of our history is divided between BC and AD – before Christ lived or after his birth. Fairy stories just couldn't exert this kind of lasting, global influence on our calendar.

Many of the people who wrote the New Testament died because they refused to deny their faith in Jesus. But why die for a lie? Why not just say, 'Sorry, chaps, big mistake, we made the whole thing up'?

Even if we dismiss the Bible's evidence for Jesus' existence, we can still discover his presence in other early writings. In AD 52 a man called Thalles mentioned Jesus' crucifixion in his account of the history of the Mediterranean world, and tried to provide an explanation for the darkness that had occurred at the same time (see Luke 23:44,45) as his death. In AD 112 Pliny, a governor in a Roman province, wrote a letter to the emperor of the day asking for advice on how to deal with Jesus' followers. In AD 115 Tacitus, a Roman historian, wrote about 'those who are commonly called Christians', recording that 'Christus, from whom their name is derived, was executed at the hands of the procurator Pontius Pilate in the reign of Tiberius' (Tacitus, *Annals*, XV 44.2-8). Probably the clearest report on the early Christian church comes from Josephus, a Jewish general living in exile in Rome. Towards the end of the first century he wrote a treatise outlining the history of the Jews, and in one part of this history he described Jesus in some detail:

> Now, there was about this time Jesus, a wise man, if it be lawful to call him a man, for he was a doer of wonderful works, a teacher of such men as received the truth with pleasure. He drew over to him both many of the Jews and many of the Gentiles. He was the Christ.

And when Pilate had condemned him to the cross, those that loved him at the first did not forsake him; for he appeared to them alive again at the third day; as the divine prophet had foretold these and ten thousand other wonderful things concerning him. And the tribe of Christians, so named from him, are not extinct at this day. (*The Antiquities of the Jews*, XVIII, 33)

Not one of these men had Christian sympathies. Jesus was a problem they could have lived without. But they couldn't ignore him because they were historians and he was a fact of history. He was a flesh-and-blood first-century man. Just as real as Nelson, Napoleon or Winston Churchill.

Who was Jesus?

That Jesus actually lived is clear, but what kind of person was he? All the different suggestions that have been made boil down to four basic options.

A good man?

A quick survey of the people in your place of work will reveal how popular this view is, and it's not difficult to see why. The Gospels – the accounts of the life of Jesus recorded by Matthew, Mark, Luke and John in the Bible – show Jesus as kind and considerate, keen to help people, especially the underprivileged; a man who wanted to right wrongs and see justice done, to bring peace and joy, to replace unrest and sadness.

So far so good, but it's only half the story. Alongside all this niceness, he kept on saying and doing things which good men couldn't or wouldn't say or do! Eyewitnesses saw him walk on water, heal people, calm a storm and raise people from the dead. He said the kinds of things that even the most conceited big-head would never dare say; such as, 'If you believe in me you will live for ever' and 'I am the only way to get to God'. He claimed to be able to forgive sins and talk directly to God whom he called his father. He said that he had been given all the power in the universe and had always been in existence! He challenged an angry crowd to find a single sin in his life – and they couldn't! And he was happy to let people worship him.

Now think of some of the really good people you know or have heard about. It's hard to imagine Mother Teresa saying that she had always been in existence, or Nelson Mandela offering you eternal life! There have been hundreds of good people over the years, yet not a single one of them (precisely because they were good) would have dreamed of saying the things Jesus did. The same is true of all the religious teachers in history – Confucius, Buddha, Socrates, Muhammad. None of them ever made these kinds of claims. Good people don't, and the people who encountered Jesus knew this. In the New Testament we meet those who loved Jesus and those who hated him; very few sat on the fence and remained indifferent. This was because what he said was so shocking. As shocking as the Pope appearing on television and claiming to be God. No, the 'good man' option simply doesn't fit the facts.

A mad man?

I *have* met people who made claims like those Jesus made. Some claimed to be God himself, some only that they were his special messenger, and others that they had supernatural powers. All these people were in institutions that care for the mentally ill! Perhaps Jesus ought to be included with them, as just another well-meaning but deluded lunatic? Was he sincere but unbalanced? Let's look at the evidence:

His **character** – Jesus was patient with his followers and kind to children. He always appeared in control of himself and the situation. He was always compassionate and ready to respond to cries for help.

His **teaching** – Jesus gave clear, cohesive statements about life-and-death issues and well-illustrated guidelines for human behaviour. His statements about God had a depth and perception that are simply light years ahead of anyone else in religious literature.

His **relationships** – Jesus was a loyal son, a faithful friend and a fearless leader.

His **abilities** – Jesus was superb in public debate, demolishing his opponents' arguments with rapier-like thrusts of logic. He was skilled at relating to people at any level of society, and aware of his greatness without a trace of pomposity.

If all this describes madness, may I be struck down with it immediately! In fact, Jesus' personality and the power of his message point to a profound sanity. Which brings us to option three.

A bad man?

What if Jesus was just a con-man? A liar who deceived people into believing his message?

This argument supposes that people in the first century were idiots. Some would have been fooled, of course, but sooner or later Jesus would have been rumbled. Yet throughout his entire life no one was ever able to expose him as a fraud or discover inconsistencies between what he said and the way he lived. Everything we know about his life – his moral purity, his deep concerns, his teaching – simply doesn't add up to a description of a manipulative schemer. To believe that Jesus was such a superb con-man that he could demonstrate such good qualities and maintain them consistently, fool every close friend and then be willing to die to keep up the fraud, would stretch the imagination to breaking point. There is not a single piece of evidence that shows him to be deceiving, manipulating or lying. And Jesus was poor throughout his life and penniless at his death.

Before we move on to option four, let's look at the implications of our discussion so far. Each of the first three options could be true about part of Jesus' life. For instance, if we had a record only of his kind actions, the 'good man' option would fit the facts perfectly. If we only had his wild claims to be God, no one would argue with the 'mad man' tag. If we only had his promises without any fulfilment, 'bad man' would be written against his name without hesitation. But we have a diversity of information about Jesus and we must examine all of it.

A blind man was asked to describe an elephant after only feeling its tail. 'An elephant is like a rope,' he said, confidently. But an examination of all the data (the trunk, head, shoulders, etc) would show that the man was wrong – an elephant is nothing like a rope. Far too many descriptions of Jesus are pretty ropey! They don't do justice to the person who is revealed when we examine all the evidence about him.

A God-man?

This fourth option would be that Jesus was a very special human being and that he was also God. Completely human and completely divine. God and man in the same person. True, this is a staggering statement. But, however remarkable it appears, it fits the facts we have better than anything else.

Hardly anyone would dispute the first part of this option; Jesus was very special. Thousands of thinking people have written or spoken about his impact on our world. Statesmen, philosophers, scientists, poets and leaders in every sphere of society, Christians and non-Christians, those writing in history and those speaking today, academics from every discipline – all have acknowledged the massive impact this first-century Jew has had on our planet. This anonymous prose-poem about Jesus sums it up well:

> He was born in an obscure village, the child of a peasant woman. He grew up in yet another village, where he worked in a carpenter's shop till he was 30. Then for three years he was an itinerant preacher.
>
> He never wrote a book. He never held an office. He never had a family or owned a house. He didn't go to college. He never visited a big city. He never travelled more than 200 miles from the place where he was born. He did none of the things one usually associates with greatness. He had no credentials but himself.
>
> He was only 33 when the tide of public opinion turned against him. His friends ran away. He was nailed to a cross between two thieves. While he was dying, his executioners gambled for his clothing, the only property he had on earth.

Twenty centuries have come and gone and today he is the central figure of the human race. All the armies that ever marched, all the navies that ever sailed, all the parliaments that ever sat, all the kings that ever reigned, put together, have not affected the life of man on this earth as much as that one solitary life!

No question about it, Jesus was unique. But was he – is he – God?

Well, he certainly claimed to be. He took the special Hebrew name for God and used it of himself. He didn't stop people worshipping him. He forgave sins and raised the dead. He said that to receive him was to receive God!

Peter thought that Jesus was God ('You are the Messiah, the Son of the living God', Matthew 16:16) and so did Thomas ('You are my Lord and my God!' John 20:28). Paul, John, Stephen and John the Baptist made clear statements about his divinity (Romans 1:3,4; John 1:1–14; Acts 7:54–56; John 1:32–34). The reason his enemies wanted to get rid of him was because he claimed he was equal to God ('You are just a man, and here you are claiming to be God!' John 10:33). The early Christian church was in no doubt, either: the leader of the whole Roman empire was made aware of their belief in Jesus' divinity in a letter from Pliny. Referring to Christians, Pliny wrote, 'They were in the habit of meeting on a fixed day before it was light, when they sang in alternate verse a hymn to Christ as a God' (Pliny to Trajan, *Epp.* X 96).

The early church thought Jesus was God, and Christians continue to believe it today. Even a battle-hardened general, Napoleon, is recorded as saying, 'I think I understand something of human nature, and I tell you none else is like him; Jesus Christ was more than man.' After a description of Jesus' incredible authority, Napoleon concludes, 'This it is which proves to me quite convincingly the divinity of Jesus Christ' (from a conversation quoted by H P Lydon in *The Divinity of our Lord and Saviour, Jesus Christ*, Rivingtons).

So a great deal of testimony points to Jesus being both God and man. Now, we are not saying that this is an easy proposition to take on board; just that it makes the most sense of all the data available. It is horrendously difficult to imagine God and man in the same person, but it would be quite wrong to reject this option simply because it blows our minds. Scientists tell us that two theories are needed to explain how light works – one theory says that light is made up of particles, the other that it consists of waves. Neither theory on its own is enough to explain what light is; both are needed. Yet science has still not discovered how the two work together. It defies the imagination. However, scientists have accepted both theories because they are the best explanation of the facts we have. Similarly, we cannot explain how God and man could both be present in the person of Jesus. However, a thorough, open appraisal of everything Jesus said and did leads to this conclusion. No other theory comes anywhere close to accounting for all the facts we know about Jesus of Nazareth.

Did Jesus rise from the dead?

On Easter Sunday 1996 the BBC's *Heart of the Matter* series screened a programme claiming to have unearthed 'remarkable archaelogical evidence' for the discovery of Jesus' bones. A number of caskets and burial urns, labelled with names like 'Mary', 'Joseph' and 'Jesus', had been excavated in Jerusalem and, it was argued, these sensational 'finds' proved conclusively once and for all that Jesus' resurrection never happened.

Christian scholars have given a robust response to the programme's claims. The names Mary, Joseph and Jesus were extremely common at that time, and this material was dug up in the 1980s so the discovery isn't exactly new. Recent reports in a Palestinian newspaper have also suggested that the characters written on the caskets don't necessarily say what was claimed. Even more telling was the lack of interest shown by archaeologists, who would have loved to have been able to show that Jesus was well and truly buried. At best, all that can be established is that this was the mortuary of a first-century middle-class family from Jerusalem.

The claims made by *Heart of the Matter* were not the first nor the most recent in a long line of attacks on the truth of the resurrection. What are we to make of them? Can we trust the Bible's accounts of the resurrection, or is it all sheer fiction, dreamed up by his followers to bolster a failing cause and believed in by millions of gullible people ever since? The resurrection of Jesus lies at the heart of the Christian faith. In a letter to the new church he had established in Corinth, the apostle Paul writes:

> ... if Christ wasn't raised to life, our message is worthless, and so is your faith. If the dead won't be raised to life, we have told lies about God by saying that he raised Christ to life, when he really did not. So if the dead won't be raised to life, Christ wasn't raised to life. Unless Christ was raised to life, your faith is useless, and you are still living in your sins. And those people who died after putting their faith in him are completely lost. If our hope in Christ is good only for this life, we are worse off than anyone else.
>
> 1 Corinthians 15:14–19

Of course, if Jesus was God, coming back to life again wouldn't be a problem. But let's pause and take a summary of the Bible's account of what happened.

Jesus was betrayed by a close associate, tried by the Jews, handed over to the Romans and executed by crucifixion. After his death he was placed in a tomb provided by a wealthy supporter. On the morning after the Sabbath some women came to visit his grave, only to discover that he was not dead any more – but alive.

Dead men usually don't come back to life, so some people have a hard time with the simple statement in the Gospels, 'He is risen'. A number of alternative possibilities have been suggested.

'Jesus never really died'

Perhaps Jesus revived in the tomb and then went to the disciples to give them his final instructions? This theory asks us to believe that a man who had been brutally beaten, strung up on a cross for six hours with nails in his hands and feet, and who had a spear rammed into his side, is still alive. Then, after at least 36 hours in a cold tomb, he unwrapped himself from yards of cloth soaked in 34 kilograms of spice, pushed away a stone so huge that three women could not budge it, fought his way past the guard, walked miles on nail-damaged feet and appeared to his disciples as a picture of health, the conqueror of death! Enough said! You would need to be more gullible than King Canute to believe that.

'Somebody moved the body'

But who? Not the Jewish or Roman authorities, that's for sure. In less than six weeks all Jerusalem was buzzing with rumours about Jesus being alive. Within three months the rumours had become a tidal wave of popular opinion, resulting in acute embarrassment for the authorities. Religious values were being challenged and revolution was in the air; and all on the basis of Jesus being alive. All this could have been stopped in its tracks if the body had been produced. Why wasn't it? Because the authorities did not have it.

It is equally difficult to argue that Jesus' followers stole his body. The chances of this timorous group thinking up this idea, overpowering the guards and hiding the body so brilliantly it was never discovered, are extremely remote. And you would have to explain why they then went on to risk death on the basis of a lie. It's hard to believe the disciples would spend the rest of their lives living as though Jesus were alive when they knew his body was actually rotting away in some unmarked Galilean grave. No, this explanation causes more problems than it solves.

'The disciples hallucinated'

People do have hallucinations; they see or hear things which are not really there. However, what we have in the evidence before us

seems to exclude this possibility. Jesus appeared on a dozen
occasions, to individuals and groups of his followers, in very different locations. Once he appeared to a crowd of over 500
people. And these were not fleeting glimpses, here one minute
and gone the next; they were often prolonged interviews.
Hallucinations are usually a result of some kind of wish-fulfil-
ment, but the disciples themselves took some convincing! The
resurrection was a complete surprise to them.

In addition to the three explanations outlined above, other
more fanciful options have been suggested: robbers stole the
body; the women went to the wrong tomb; they crucified the
wrong man. All these are selective in their use of the facts, and a
cursory glance reveals what empty explanations they are, particularly in the light of what went on soon after Jesus had died and
has continued right up to the present day.

Look what happened to the disciples! They were transformed
from a terrified rabble into a cemented group who fearlessly pro-
claimed their message. They healed the sick, won debates with
Jewish academics and went gladly to cruel deaths for their
beliefs. What on earth brought about such an amazing change?

Look what happened to the new believers, the church!
Beginning soon after Jesus' death, its impact was incredible.
Three thousand people, then five thousand, then a large number
of Jewish priests were won over to become followers of Jesus. The
Christian message spread like wildfire in the ancient world.
Down the centuries the church has been persecuted and ridiculed, yet it still continues to go from strength to strength. What
event could have triggered off the start of this enduring institution?

Look what happened to the Sabbath! It got changed to
Sunday! Remember, most of the disciples were Jews brought up
to observe the Sabbath (Saturday). It was one of the most fer-
vently held tenets of Judaism, a centuries-old custom which was
absolutely binding on every Jew. What happened to cause this
major break with tradition if it wasn't the desire to celebrate the
resurrection of Jesus on the first day of the week?

All these things point to some stupendous event. If not the

resurrection, then what? No other satisfactory explanation has been put forward. The evidence in favour of it is convincing. A former Lord Chief Justice of England, Lord Darling, said of the resurrection, 'In its favour as a living truth there exists such overwhelming evidence, positive and negative, factual and circumstantial, that no intelligent jury in the world could fail to bring in a verdict that the resurrection story is true.'

The resurrection of Jesus is at the heart of the Christian faith. If you could produce an alternative theory which more completely explained all the evidence, I would have to be honest enough to abandon my Christian faith. On the other hand, if you can't, surely you will be honest enough to follow this evidence to its logical conclusion – the resurrection of Jesus really happened!

5

Can I trust the Bible?

No one in their right mind would doubt that the Bible is a remarkable book. It has long been the number one bestseller. Each year people buy hundreds of millions of Bibles. The Bible – the whole book or part of it – is available in over two thousand languages, and each year sees yet more translations. And all this despite the fact that the Bible is no lightweight paperback novel. Not exactly easy reading!

There are always plenty of people around trying to dispute the validity of the Bible. But whether it's trustworthy or not is such an important issue that it's worth investigating it yourself and settling the matter rather than being swayed by other people's contradictory opinions.

The Bible is not a single book but a collection of 66 books, written by about 40 authors, using over three-quarters of a million words, over a period spanning more than a thousand years. And there is an amazing harmony in it from beginning to end!

The Bible has been the most discussed, debated and quoted book in history. Abraham Lincoln said of it, 'I believe the Bible is the best gift God has given to man', and hundreds of statesmen since have paid tribute to its value. Charles Dickens described the New Testament as 'the very best book that ever was or ever will be known in the world', and countless authors since have drawn their inspiration from its pages. Millions of ordinary men and women, from every background and occupation, have found strength and guidance in its teaching. Yes, the Bible is certainly a remarkable book.

No thinking person will be content to leave it at that. 'Is the Bible true?' is the crucial question. After all, millions of newspapers are sold every day. Does the sheer number guarantee that they are telling the truth? Hardly! So the vast quantity of Bibles doesn't guarantee the truthfulness of what the book says. What about all those contradictions and unbelievable miracle stories? Perhaps the writers just made up the whole thing. Did the people in the Bible stories really exist? Is there any evidence to support what the Bible says? Is it really any help to sophisticated, scientific men and women at the beginning of the third millennium?

Miracles?

Many miraculous events are certainly recorded in the Bible: the Israelites crossed the Red Sea without getting their feet wet; five thousand people enjoyed a free lunch, all from a few loaves of bread and a couple of fish; a man who had been dead for four days was brought back to life; and lots more. We can't just ignore these events; they are an essential part of the Bible. Take them away and there is no message left, because at the very heart of Christianity we find the miracle of God becoming a man in Jesus and the miracle of Jesus being raised from the dead. Without these two miracles the Christian faith falls flat on its face, becoming a set of pious platitudes supported by some common-sense advice. We would be left with a much briefer Bible but a message that had ceased to be Christianity!

We can't explain the miracles away either. Some people try, of course, by assuming that in Bible times people were ignorant, superstitious and primitive. This view disregards the evidence of history which reveals a much less naive view of the miraculous than we might expect. People may have been a little gullible and superstitious (as are many today in the sophisticated West!) but they weren't stupid! They knew just as well as we do that virgins don't give birth to babies, dead men stay dead and that walking on water is not a normal human activity. The eyewitnesses of these incidents couldn't explain what had happened, but neither could they ignore the evidence of their senses.

And they didn't give in to the evidence easily. Paul wouldn't believe a word of it until he himself met the risen Christ on the way to Damascus. Mary gave the angel a hard time before she could feel confident about the virgin birth. And Thomas the cynic said he wasn't going to fall for any of that resurrection stuff until he had some proof – real, tangible proof.

Given that this may be true, aren't miracles impossible because they break the laws of nature? Well, the laws of nature are generalisations about what *usually* happens. They don't explain *why* something happens or why it should *always* happen.

Scientific laws cannot, by definition, exclude the possibility of miracles. Of course, by their very nature, miracles are rare – but this doesn't mean they *never* take place. Remarkably improbable things *do* occur. The odds against being dealt a perfect hand in bridge are 635,013,559,600 to one – but it has happened!

Funnily enough, this business of the miraculous has become less of a problem to most people in the last quarter of the twentieth century and opening quarter of the twenty-first than for many previous generations. There has been an explosion of interest in the occult, the paranormal, the 'other'. Evidence of this is seen in television programmes like *The X-Files* or *Buffy the Vampire Slayer* achieving cult status and huge followings. Then there's the *Harry Potter* phenomenon, the revival through film of fascination with *The Lord of the Rings*, and the award-winning success of the Philip Pullman trilogy – *His Dark Materials*. Are there supernatural powers? Have real UFOs been sighted? Is there life on other planets? Does faith-healing work? Is Satan real? Can we see into the future? People have realised that science and logic don't have all the answers – and perhaps scientists have openly begun to declare the shortcomings of their data. Many thinking people are open to the possibility of forces at work over which we have little or no control.

But intervention by the divine? Healings, transformed lives and transformed circumstances in answer to prayer? Christians claim that miracles do occur today. I know literally dozens of people who can point to an event in their lives which they simply cannot explain in any way other than by using the word 'miracle'. I am not talking about emotionally unstable or gullible people – we have to take their evidence seriously.

If anyone decides in advance that miracles cannot occur, then no amount of evidence will convince them otherwise! But for the genuine, honest enquirer, the miracles of the Bible – however baffling – need not be a barrier to discovering the message that lies at its heart.

Contradictions?

Sooner or later, whenever there is a discussion about the Bible, someone will comment on all the *contradictions* in it. Often what they say isn't a question – 'How can you believe a book so full of contradictions?' – but a confident statement: 'The Bible is full of contradictions.' I have a suspicion that the vast majority of people who say this have never read the Bible thoroughly. The Bible is often treated like a dictionary – most homes have one, but hardly anyone uses it. We would rather ask a friend how to spell a word than look it up ourselves. But though this method is quicker, it is much less reliable. Lots of people get their knowledge of the Bible this way – second-hand. So many of those who make dogmatic statements about the inconsistencies in the Bible are simply repeating well-worn clichés handed on to them by someone else. When asked to produce even *one* of these supposed contradictions, they are usually at a complete loss!

Here is another dogmatic statement, and I would like to produce some evidence to support it: 'The Bible is not full of contradictions.' I have read the Bible from start to finish and some parts of it many times. I have discovered quite a few things that *seemed* to contradict each other. These were all relatively incidental things, certainly not anything which remotely affected the message of the book. And where there have been what seemed like inconsistencies, as I came to understand more about ancient languages and Jewish culture, and delved deeper into the biblical text, I found that these inconsistencies disappeared.

I'm not the only one. Thousands of serious scholars have given much of their lives to in-depth study of the Bible and have emerged with greater confidence in its reliability. One of these academics, Dr Gleason Archer (Professor of Semitic studies at Trinity Evangelical Divinity School, Illinois), has put together a book that deals with almost all these alleged inconsistencies. In the preface to the book he writes:

As I have dealt with one apparent discrepancy after another and have studied the alleged contradictions between the biblical record and the evidence of linguistics, archaeology, or science, my confidence in the trustworthiness of scripture has been repeatedly verified and strengthened by the discovery that almost every problem in scripture that had ever been discovered by man, from ancient times until now, has been dealt with in a completely satisfactory manner by the biblical text itself – or else by objective archaeological information. (*Encyclopaedia of Bible Difficulties*, Zondervan, 1990.)

Don't take Dr Archer's word on this, or mine; find out for yourself. If you read the Bible with an open mind, I think you're going to come to the same conclusion.

A message from God to be trusted?

The Bible claims to be God's message to the world. I want to give five reasons why I think that this is a genuine claim – five pieces of evidence which make me confident that the Bible is absolutely trustworthy and will always be relevant.

Manuscripts

A large part of the Bible deals with eyewitness accounts – firsthand information passed on with meticulous care. Even today the Jewish people repeat their traditional teaching and stories in the same form as they did centuries ago. Besides, all the New Testament books were written down within 40 years after Jesus died. Just think how hard it would be to describe the years after the Second World War as a time of 'plentiful petrol, no rationing, hardly any bomb damage in London and plenty of money for everyone'. There are thousands of people still alive today who would say you were lying. They were there! So, when the New Testament books were first circulating, there would have been uproar if the facts were inaccurate or simply made up.

When the first manuscripts were copied, they weren't done in some cavalier, haphazard fashion. The Jewish copyists took their work seriously. The discovery of even the smallest error could lead to the whole manuscript being destroyed and work beginning all over again. There are thousands of these copies available to study, and they give us a remarkably accurate picture of the original documents. This is what makes the Bible unique.

There are simply no other writings from this period with anything like the support the Bible has. Everyone believes that Julius Caesar came to Britain in 55 BC, but we only have nine or ten manuscripts to support this and the earliest was written 900 years after the event! In contrast, we have over 2000 manuscripts of the Gospels, some of which were written only 200 years after the event. As time goes by, earlier manuscripts come to light which confirm the accuracy of later copies. (The oldest fragment of a manuscript we have discovered so far can be seen in the John Ryland University Library, Manchester, England. It is dated AD 130 – only a few decades after the original was written!) All in all, the manuscript evidence is impressive:

> The wealth of manuscripts, and above all the narrow interval of time between the writing and the earliest extant copies, make it by far the best attested text of any ancient writing in the world. (From *Can we Trust the New Testament?* by John Robinson, Mowbray, an imprint of Cassell plc.)

So what we have in the Bible is a very well documented, carefully compiled piece of literature; an authentic record of events, preserved over the centuries with unequalled accuracy. It cannot be dismissed lightly.

Archaeology

Digging around in ancient ruins is not everyone's idea of a good time, but this painstaking and detailed work has produced compelling evidence to support the accuracy of many Bible passages. Time after time, those who question the integrity of the Bible have to retreat in the face of clear archaeological evidence.

In the late nineteenth century, archaelogical investigator Sir William Ramsay went to the Middle East expecting to discover evidence confirming the inaccuracies of the Bible. He found precisely the opposite! Everything he uncovered showed how reliable the biblical record was. Others have discovered this since. Donald Wiseman, professor emeritus at London University, writes: 'No fact of archaeology so far discovered contradicts the biblical record' (*Digging for Truth*, Viewpoint No. 31, Inter School Christian Fellowship). And Dr J O Kinnaman writes: 'Of the hundreds of thousands of artefacts found by the archaeologists, not one has ever been discovered that contradicts or denies one word, phrase, clause or sentence of the Bible.' (*The Encyclopaedia of 7700 Illustrations*, Assurance.)

From as long ago as 2000 BC there is archaeological evidence that confirms many of the details given in the Bible: facts about the city Abraham came from; the unearthing of some of Solomon's military installations; inscriptions from the time of Moses; remarkable confirmation that the Jews really did go into exile in the sixth century BC. Turning to the New Testament, scholars had dismissed as 'poetic licence' John's description of the Pool of Bethesda in chapter five of his Gospel. But in 1888 archaeologists excavated the site and discovered all five porches and an inscription saying that the water had healing properties! Luke has also been confirmed as a reliable historian and Paul as an accurate author.

All this should help us get away from the idea that the Bible is a collection of fairy tales, a sort of spiritual *Aesop's Fables*. It isn't. It's a message with its roots in history and its basis in fact.

Prophecy

Another thing that makes the Bible such an amazing book is the way it predicts events in the future, which then happen. I don't mean the sort of thing you can read in your average horoscope – 'Today you will meet a handsome stranger. Tomorrow it will be dry if it's not raining.' I mean specific predictions which are unmistakably fulfilled. There are hundreds of them in the Bible.

Ezekiel predicted in the sixth century BC that Tyre (a major city and thriving industrial centre) would be defeated and utterly destroyed. Nebuchadnezzar and then Alexander the Great brought about the fulfilment of this prophecy in 333 BC. It even says in Ezekiel 26:14, 'I will leave only a bare rock where fishermen can dry their nets.' Sure enough, after Tyre was taken over by the Arabs in AD 1291, it became a poor fishing village. Among many other fulfilled predictions, Amos foretold the downfall of Israel, Jeremiah the capture of Jerusalem, Isaiah the return of the Jews from exile, and Jesus the destruction of Jerusalem.

Jesus' own coming to earth was predicted in a precise way. He was to be born in Bethlehem (Micah 5:2). He would enter Jerusalem on a donkey (Zechariah 9:9), be rejected and killed (Isaiah 53:3-5), while men gambled for his clothes (Psalm 22:18). All these predictions were made over 400 years before Jesus came. Each one happened. In fact, not a single prediction in the Bible can be shown to be false – a remarkable record.

Survival under attack

The Bible has had its enemies, yet it has resisted all their attacks, and its influence continues to grow. This is even more remarkable when you consider the nature of the opposition.

There has been opposition from philosophers, some of whom have relegated the Bible to the level of ancient superstition, a set of ideas appropriate to the dawn of civilisation but irrelevant to our advancing culture. The eighteenth-century French thinker Voltaire predicted that the Bible's days were numbered, and an enlightened world would soon discard it as more advanced, rational philosophies would take over. But, over 200 years after his death, the Bible is more widely read than ever before. The ironic thing is, Voltaire's old house in France is now used as a storage and distribution centre for a Bible agency!

There has been opposition from governments. From time to time, over the last 2000 years of Christianity, the Bible has been outlawed. During the French Revolution it was seen as an instrument of aristocratic oppression, and owning or reading a Bible was officially discouraged. Jean-Jacques Rousseau's *Social*

Contract (1762) was seen as a much more significant piece of literature for the salvation of France. In the twentieth century we saw the rise and fall of atheistic Communism, particularly in Russia and China. Millions of people have lived under governments that actively discouraged the ownership and reading of the Bible. Printing presses were destroyed and printers put in prison. If spoken of at all, the Bible was dismissed as capitalist propaganda unworthy of consideration in the new world of the revolution. But, after decades of attack, there is still a great demand for Bibles in the former Soviet Union. More and more young people in Eastern Europe want to read it for themselves and many Christian groups are crying out to the West for more Bibles to meet growing demand. Similar things are happening in China. What is certain is that years of government pressure have not dented the Bible's defences. If anything, its popularity grows.

There has even been opposition from inside the church – well, sections of it anyway! As long ago as the fourteenth century, John Wycliffe faced vigorous opposition from the church authorities when he set to work to translate the Bible into English and make it accessible to ordinary people. Over the years liberal theologians have tried to discredit the accuracy of the biblical record, labelling the Gospels, for example, as clever stories which came largely from the imagination of the writers.

However, where we *can* check the details of the stories with outside sources, the Bible proves accurate. For example, Josephus confirms the ministry of John the Baptist, the death of Herod Agrippa and Pilate's role in the death of Jesus. All these events were historical facts, known and recorded because they happened. What's more, the 'clever stories' theory is rejected by many experts in the field of literature. C S Lewis lectured in English Literature for almost 40 years at both Oxford and Cambridge universities. After examining many different kinds of literature, he was convinced there are only two possible views of the Gospels: either they are reports of actual events, or someone came up with the modern novel-writing technique over 1500 before anyone else! He found the second view incredible. Evidence from literature studies and historical sources seems to say that statements in the Bible are reliable accounts of real events.

Opposition to the Bible continues. New theories arise that question its accuracy. Some public figures pour scorn on it. Television documentaries attempt to discredit it with half-baked opinions cloaked in the veneer of academic respectability. People cast doubt on its capacity to provide a single, coherent explanation about us and our world. But if the Bible can take the worst that the last 2000 years has thrown at it and still flourish, it seems unlikely to be in danger from any twenty-first century critic. About as much danger as a tank being damaged by a pea-shooter!

It works!

This is the crux of the matter. The four areas of evidence outlined so far all point to the reliability of the Bible, but this one brings the issue home. The Bible makes sense of the world, provides an explanation for what has gone wrong and gives a blueprint for change. And this blueprint works. Millions of people – and this is no exaggeration – have read the Bible and found that it was like looking into a mirror. Everything it said about human nature was true about them. This discovery is very depressing because the Bible has no qualms about describing the mess we are in – steeped in greed, pride, envy, lust and selfishness of every kind. No sugary coating on this bitter pill! What makes it even harder to swallow is that no one escapes judgement, no one at all.

But it is not all bad news. The Bible does go on to describe the antidote to all this – a clean sheet, wrong things forgiven and a new power for living. I have experienced this myself and have found the message of the Bible to be true.

None of this will come as a surprise to anyone who accepts what the Bible says about itself. It claims to be a message from God to every human being; no wonder what it says is true and really works in changing people's lives. You can always test this claim for yourself. Get hold of a contemporary translation of the Bible and turn to the Gospel of John. Read it carefully and with an open mind. Persevere to the end of the Gospel and keep asking yourself, 'What response do I need to make if this is true?' Ask a Christian you know to explain any bits you can't understand. If you don't know any Christians, make an appointment to see your local pastor, minister or vicar – they won't bite your head off! You will discover for yourself what a powerful book the Bible is.

6

Science and faith – fatal encounter?

Science rules OK! This could easily be the slogan that summed up the second half of the twentieth century. Science and technology (the practical application of science) dominated our world more and more. In the work-place: email and the information super-highway of the Internet. In the hospital: new drugs, microsurgery, computerised diagnostic apparatus and a bewildering array of monitoring devices. And this dependence on technology to solve our problems and cosset our daily lives continues into the twenty-first century. On our streets: cars that talk ('I need oil!') built by robots that don't, though they may one day. In our homes: television sets that pay the gas bill or buy airline tickets to the US at the touch of a button. Science fiction is rapidly becoming science fact.

As science answers more and more questions, it is inevitable that some have come to believe that science can answer the ultimate questions of life. After all, science has progressed amazingly in finding out about human beings, the beginnings of life on our planet and the origins of the universe. But is it really on the way to providing an answer to *all* our questions? Scientists have been found to be as prone to human failure, bias and temptation as anyone else, and scientific achievements are responsible for creating as many problems as solutions. Modern technology is used to produce ever more deadly weapons. Think of the advances in the nuclear arsenals of many countries, the development of the 'smart' bomb and terrifying array of chemical and biological weapons available today. Think of the casualties of accidents such as the Chernobyl disaster and conflicts such as the Gulf War. It's hardly surprising that people are left wondering whether scientific progress is progress at all and whether the human race is mature enough to ensure that scientific discoveries are not misused. And, also unsurprising, there has been a backlash against rational, scientific thinking as people find ever more esoteric religious beliefs to satisfy their hunger for the mystical and the spiritual, which science isn't able to offer.

However, well-known scientists like Stephen Hawking and Richard Dawkins raise doubt in the public mind about God's role in creation and whether it is credible to hold any kind of religious belief. We are often told that science and religion are in conflict, and not left in much doubt about which is wrong! 'People *used* to believe that, but science has shown it not to be true.' End of contest. A knock-out victory for science over faith in the first round.

But has science really sounded the death-knell for Christianity? Is Christianity bound for the scrap heap of history – a belief that was all right for our superstitious ancestors, but no use to modern scientific man? If this is so, let's be honest enough to leave it behind and move on to scientific maturity. However, is this simplistic view of the relationship between science and faith accurate? Let's look at the three main areas where the conflict is supposed to be most fierce.

Conflict in history?

Some people argue that Christianity and science have always been in conflict. And history throws up some colourful debates for illustration:

• Didn't Galileo get into trouble with the church authorities for saying that the earth revolved around the sun? Weren't the church authorities outraged because his scientific proofs upset their view that the earth was the centre of everything and all the other planets and stars revolved around it?

- Then there was that famous debate in 1860 between scientist and humanist T H Huxley and Bishop Wilberforce, in which the cleric ridiculed the scientific view of evolution by asking Huxley whether he was related to a monkey through his grandmother or his grandfather! This exchange produced more heat than light, and the scientific community accused the Church of being completely closed to reasonable discussion.

- What about Bishop Ussher in the seventeenth century, who used the Bible to calculate that the world came into existence on October 18 and that man was made at nine o'clock in the morning on October 23, in 4004 BC?

Whenever the subject of science or faith crops up – in television documentaries, textbooks, discussion with science students – these three illustrations are trotted out to 'prove' that conflict exists. But if this conflict is as obvious as some people say it is, why aren't there dozens and dozens of examples to demonstrate it instead of the same tired handful? After all, modern scientific enquiry has been around for over 400 years – surely time enough for the conflict to have escalated into all-out war and for one side to have sent the other packing! There are, of course, other examples of conflict between scientific and religious establishments than the ones mentioned, but on the whole they are surprisingly rare.

There is simply no compelling evidence that Christianity has ever 'had it in for' science. Even the supposedly cast-iron illustrations outlined above are open to debate. Perhaps the Wilberforce-Huxley conflict tells us as much about a scientific community which thought itself above contradiction as it does about an opinionated bishop with a sense of humour! And not every theologian and church leader agreed with Ussher's dates for the creation of the world: in fact, there was as much opposition to his findings from inside the Church as outside.

More seriously, there doesn't seem to be any real evidence that the Galileo story happened as is so often related. An examination of the facts is difficult because of incomplete documentation, but such evidence as there is shows substantial differences from the popular story. The idea that the earth was not the centre of the planetary system was not new. Polish astronomer Nicolaus Copernicus had said the same thing a hundred years earlier and did not get into big trouble with the Church over his views. Over 30 years before Galileo's 'trial', Johannes Kepler declared openly that the earth went round the sun. Kepler was a devout follower of Luther and, after making his discoveries, was still able to assert that the universe itself was an expression of the being of God.

> ... whatever the row over Galileo was about, it was not cosmology – not really. In fact, the whole unfortunate episode arose from the Pope feeling betrayed and insulted by the way his former friend Galileo had chosen to represent his own views about cosmology. It was a silly, personal squabble – not the big science versus religion debate it was later cracked up to be. (From *Doing away with God?* by Russell Stannard, Professor of Physics at The Open University, MarshallPickering, an imprint of HarperCollins *Religious*, 1993.)

Galileo himself did not see his astronomical discoveries as discrediting the Bible, and, though he remained under house arrest for the rest of his life, he was not prevented by the Church from continuing his scientific investigation. After his trial he went on to make his most significant contribution to science in the field of dynamics. Hungarian author Arthur Koestler, who was certainly not a supporter of Christianity, said that it is quite wrong to see the Galileo incident as a 'show-down between "blind faith" and "enlightened reason",' (*The Sleepwalkers*, Pelican, 1959).

All in all, none of these three incidents gives us good evidence of any continuing conflict between science and religion through history. In fact, whenever there is conflict it seems to me to be the exception rather than the rule. Certainly we would expect this to be so when we realise that the rise of modern science can be linked to biblical Christianity. Many of the first scientists were Christians – among them Francis Bacon, Isaac Newton and Robert Boyle – as the Christian worldview encouraged careful investigation of the universe God had made. It was in this atmosphere that modern scientific enquiry was born.

Far from being an enemy, science was in fact a product of thoughtful Christianity. From the birth of science to the present day there is no cohesive evidence to demonstrate that Christian faith and scientific enquiry are in opposition. Indeed, renowned novelist Susan Howatch seems to have thought that the two had enough in common for her to endow Cambridge University with a lectureship in Theology and Natural Science.

Conflict in principle?

Aren't science and Christianity poles apart in their basic stance? Doesn't one deal in facts and the other in faith? Doesn't one give proof and the other ask for belief? Hasn't science done away with the need for faith? Let's examine what science actually *is*.

Science makes observations, carries out experiments, formulates hypotheses, tests them, defines them and then produces a theory which it believes best explains the facts. It is trying to get at the truth about *how* our world works. But science only offers one aspect of the truth. For example, as a scientist you could say that playing the violin was 'rubbing the entrails of a dead sheep with the hairs of a dead horse', and you would be describing the facts accurately – but not all the facts. You would not be answering the question of why certain sounds are harmonious and others not, why the music is enjoyable or why the violinist is playing at all. Strictly speaking, science can only answer the 'how' questions, not the 'why' questions.

This is an important fact to grasp. To the question 'Why is the grass burning?' a scientist could answer by talking about the presence of oxygen, the combustible nature of grass, wind factors, and so on. But this is actually a description of *what* is occurring, not an explanation of *why*. The answer to the 'why' question could be a carelessly discarded cigarette, a farmer clearing his waste ground or a malicious prankster! It is precisely in the 'why' area that Christianity has so much to say. Science cannot help us with issues like right and wrong, beauty, peace, joy and love – they are simply outside its scope. These subjects do not yield their secrets to the laboratory or the study. God cannot be put under a microscope or the Christian faith examined in a test tube. These things are beyond the realm of scientific enquiry.

So we have established that science and Christianity are different in that they answer different questions. But there is an important point of similarity. Both are based on faith! (Scientists call them presuppositions, but they can't be scientifically proved and so are really statements of faith.) Now this comes as quite a shock to a lot of people who think that science is all about facts. In reality, all science is based on at least two statements of faith:

- The universe is an orderly place, which works on a uniform, regular basis.
- The information received by our senses and minds is an accurate picture of the universe.

Now it is absolutely impossible to 'prove' either of these statements scientifically. Yet if you don't accept them, there is no point bothering with scientific investigation. If, for example, the second statement wasn't true, science would be like trying to receive television programmes on a set with no aerial. The screen would be blurred at best, blank at worst. If your senses only perceive the universe in this kind of way, science becomes a cosmic guessing game of little practical relevance. What we actually believe is that our scientific aerial is secure and, as we continue to tune our science in, we get a clearer and clearer picture of what the universe is like. Neither of these two beliefs of science can, however, be proved any more than 'there is a God' or 'Jesus died for me' can be proved scientifically.

Science and Christianity are both based on assumptions that cannot be proved. Perhaps this fact ought to make us a little more cautious about the dogmatic statements of some scientists and a little more open to examine the claims of Christianity.

One of the most convincing reasons for not seeing any real conflict in principle between science and Christianity is a practical one. So many scientists today *are* Christians!

Intelligent men and women in every field of scientific research see absolutely no conflict between what they believe as scientists and what they believe as Christians. For example:

> If I didn't believe that I had a God who was solid and dependable, a God who makes no mistakes, I couldn't continue what I'm doing. I think the hallmark of my existence is the integration of my surgical life with my Christian faith. (Dr C Everett Koop, former Surgeon General of the United States of America.)

> I can claim that I have made several discoveries in my field, but none of them compares with the greatest discovery I have ever made. That

happened in December 1958, when I discovered that Christ was indeed my Saviour, Lord and God – and not only my Saviour but the Saviour of the whole world. (Dr Robert Selvendran, biochemist. Both quotes are from *Scientists who Believe* by Eric Barrett and David Fisher, Scripture Press, 1987.)

In addition to these two, I have statements from a professor of medical genetics, a physicist, a meteorologist, a mathematician, and about thirty other leading academics – all on my desk as I write this chapter.

These two sections have been an attempt to show that in history and in the principles they use, science and Christianity are not in conflict. The next section looks at the apparent conflict in more obvious practical areas.

Conflict in popular opinion?

I said earlier that people are increasingly sceptical about the ability of science to solve the world's problems. Although many still believe that it will be science that cures cancer and AIDS, heart disease can be prevented as much by living a healthy lifestyle as by medical intervention. New strains of quick-growing crops can indeed be used to feed the hungry, but are the rich nations developing them really all that willing to use their discoveries to help the poor without exacting a heavy price in return? Increased automation gives us extra hours of leisure and relaxation, but has also deprived many of jobs. And why, in spite of all this technological advance, are so many of us working longer and harder, and collapsing under the stress of today's working life?

Science itself is *not* really going to solve anything. Nuclear power can be used to heat our homes – or to wipe every living thing from the face of the earth. Reproductive and genetic discoveries can lead to treatment for infertile couples and the prevention of genetic disorders – or to the abortion of babies because they are disabled in some way or even, in some cultures, because they are girls. Space science might lead to a colony on the moon – or a *Star Wars*-style blood bath! It's what we *do* with our scientific progress that counts.

Despite the incredible advances in scientific knowledge in recent decades, we would be hard-pressed to show that the world has become a better place because of them. Worldwide political instability, international terrorism and the threat of a nuclear holocaust make short work of that idea. In some ways, advances in science could be regarded as extremely dangerous and part of the problem – not the solution! If a child got hold of a bow and arrow, this would be dangerous; but if a child got hold of a bomb, the consequences are unthinkable. The human race is playing with ever more lethal toys, yet hasn't enough wisdom to avoid the consequences of using them.

In spite of growing doubts about science, there is still a prevailing attitude today that though Christian belief may give people a sense of well-being or personal fulfilment, it is never going to solve our world's major dilemmas. This attitude is often based on woolly ideas of what Christianity is about: that being a Christian simply means trying to be a decent human being, obeying a lot of irrelevant rules and taking part in obsolete rituals; that Christianity has nothing to say about the real world.

But what Christianity has to say about the problems of humankind is profoundly important! Christians say that scientific advances are important, but that this progress cannot deal with the root cause of the problem – human beings themselves. As long as greed, selfishness, hatred and prejudice exist, the world's problems will not be solved by any new discovery, however wonderful it may be. Science has nothing to say about solving these basic human failings. Christians say that only a completely new start with God will begin to break the evil that lies within human nature.

Of course, Christians do not claim to be perfect people, only that they have a new power inside them to help overcome their failings. They believe that only when these fundamental issues of human nature are dealt with will we have a hope of solving the world's problems. The Christian faith offers human beings the wisdom they need to put all their new knowledge and technological advancement to the best possible use.

Perhaps the greatest conflict between science and faith in the popular mind is seen in the media. Most of us do not read scientific journals and wouldn't understand them if we did! We watch television programmes or read our newspapers, and this is where most people get their scientific information. Sadly, this information is sometimes inaccurate and often misleading. A scientific paper of any weight is hedged around with qualifications – 'given these conditions', 'other experiments pending', 'on the data available' – and is fairly tentative about reaching conclusions until much more evidence is examined. But this makes for boring television and dull articles in the press, so what we are presented with are certainties. 'Major breakthrough' and 'new discovery' sound much more exciting than the 'may be', 'possibly' and 'perhaps' of true science. This leaves your average person in the pub with the impression that definite statements of provable fact are being made.

In contrast, the Christian faith is nearly always presented in the media as being unclear, weak and contradictory. This leaves our person in the pub with the impression that there is nothing certain about Christianity, so he or she is better off believing the facts – science! This is a sad distortion of the truth, and one which is made worse by the disproportionate importance some scientists attach to their own pronouncements about everything not only inside but outside the realms of science.

Society in earlier centuries has been accused of believing everything the Church said without stopping to ask questions. By the twentieth century this role was taken over by the high priests of science! I have been amazed that still in the twenty-first century seemingly intelligent people accept without question anything done in the name of science or said by a scientist. The general public usually attach far too much weight to what scientists say, even when they are speaking about things outside their field, just because they wear the label 'scientist'.

One of the worst examples of this was during a television documentary about the beginnings of life on our planet. The presenter explained that in the past people had seen the need for a 'Great Designer' of the universe but, as science probed further and further back in time, this was becoming unnecessary.

Now this is simply nonsense. Absolute unscientific nonsense! Science can only really claim to describe processes; when scientists venture to say why these processes occur, they are heading into the realm of speculation. Science is not able to comment on whether or not God created the world. The presenter was, of course, entitled to his opinion, but not his opinion masquerading under the guise of science. The way it came over was to give what was merely his own ideas the backing of careful scientific investigation. This is misleading at best, manipulative propaganda at worst.

Another television series featured a professor of genetics examining the role of genes in the way we live and behave. One programme explored whether there was such a thing as a gene for crime, asking if it was possible to determine a 'criminal' before he or she was born, and what part science should play in controlling or eliminating these genetic 'mistakes'. At the end of the programme he visited a medieval cathedral at the edge of the French Pyrenees. A great painting covering the walls of the entire cathedral illustrates the history of the human race from creation to the Last Judgement. In the eighteenth century an arch had been pushed through the section on the Last Judgement, taking out completely the judging angel who had been weighing the souls in a pair of scales to see whether they should go to heaven or hell. The professor, himself not a religious man, commented:

> Some geneticists would like to put themselves in that arch, to judge who is saved and who is damned. The logic of genetics is that the Book of Life can be read not after death but before we're born. But to do that for crime is to deny free will to everyone, good or evil. Society, the law itself, is not the product of genes but of people, and what people do must be judged by society and not by science. (From *In the Blood*, BBC Television.)

All this means that there is a major difference in the way the general public sees science and the way it is seen by a scientist. Popular opinion may see all kinds of conflict between science and Christianity. Informed scientific opinion is likely to see much less. In general terms, whenever science speaks about areas which are scientific, conflict between it and Christianity is minimal.

What about evolution?

Of all the issues which cause concern about the relationship between science and faith, evolution has been the most explosive. 'If we evolved from the primeval slime, then God didn't make us and the book of Genesis is a fairy tale.' Well, is that true? 'Can any right-thinking person really believe in Adam and Eve?' Well, perhaps they can – given recent scientific genetic research that points to the possibility that all humanity may have evolved from a single couple! Just what is the truth about evolution?

Not all scientists believe it!

This may sound unlikely, because the impression we are given is that the entire scientific world believes in evolution and only a few eccentrics or religious cranks would deny it. The fact is that dozens of reputable scientists simply do not believe that the commonly stated evolutionary theory is the best explanation of the facts we have. I would like to quote two of them:

> I think, however, that we must go further than this and admit that the only acceptable explanation is creation. I know that this is anathema to physicists, as indeed it is to me, but we must not reject a theory that we do not like if the experimental evidence supports it. (Professor H J Lipson, *A Physicist looks at Evolution*, *Physics Bulletin* No 31, 1980.)
>
> The idea that life was put together by random shuffling of constituent molecules can be shown (in the words of Sir Fred Hoyle) to be as ridiculous and improbable as the proposition that a tornado blowing through a junk yard may assemble a Boeing 747.

The aircraft had a creator and so might life. (Professor Chandra Wickramasinghe, astronomer. From *The Lion Handbook of Christian Belief*, Lion Publishing.)

Neither of these two men, to my knowledge, are Christians. They are just unconvinced by the scientific evidence for evolution – and there are plenty of other scientists, Christian and non-Christian, who think the same. There is no need to feel embarrassed or intellectually inferior if you find creation a more viable option than evolution. It is a perfectly reasonable alternative.

Evolution is not a fact!

Evolution is a scientific theory with, it must be said, some good evidence to support it. Nevertheless, it cannot be taught as the truth. Sir Hermann Bondi, internationally acclaimed cosmologist, explains it like this:

[Evolution] is scientific precisely because it is continually subject to modification and disproof in the light of fresh insights and data accruing in numerous fields of research.

To teach it dogmatically as fact presents as erroneous a view of science as does the dogmatic teaching of physics or astronomy. If only more teaching of science stressed its human and provisional nature which is its glory! (*The Lion Handbook of Christian Belief*, Lion Publishing.)

Science is constantly on the move – refining, correcting and reviewing its theories. In the past it has held positions totally contrary to the views held today and those may change again in the future. A new discovery may open the way for a completely different idea from evolution to describe our origins.

Evolution is a description!

This is a vital fact to grasp so that we can understand the limited scope of evolution. Many people, including a large number of

Christians, have found it difficult to reconcile their belief in God with the theory of evolution. Some Christians have simply buried their heads in the sand and hoped the issue would go away. Others have come up with ludicrous statements – 'God put fossils in the ground to confuse wicked scientists!' – which are sad reflections of how far frightened people will go. Both these escapist solutions miss the point of evolution being only a description. It cannot *cause* anything. Let me explain.

If we ask the question, 'Why did the man fall from the roof?' science can draw on its resources to tell us about the mechanisms involved – the mass of the man, the velocity of the fall, gravitational pull, and so on. But this is only a description of what happened. Gravity did not *make* the man fall! To find out the cause we have to ask other questions. Did he slip? Was he pushed? Did he jump?

Similarly, evolution is a description of the way life may have started, but it cannot explain what made it start and why. Only non-scientific questions can do that. Was it chance? God? Evolution simply cannot say. This means that even if every single piece of current evolutionary theory proved accurate, it would still not rule God out of the picture.

Of course, some evolutionists *do* want to rule God out of the picture completely. They want to say that we are evolving morally as a race, moving on from our savage past to a civilised future with no need for a supreme being. Some want to use the evolutionary theory for political ends. (It is fascinating, for example, to discover that the Nazis used it to justify the mass murder of millions of Jews in World War Two!) Whenever people talk like this, they are speaking as philosophers or politicians, but not as scientists. No scientific weight can be given to their views. Christians are absolutely opposed to this misuse of science and the views (sometimes called evolutionism) which spring from it. There is, however, no inherent conflict between Christianity and *scientific* statements about evolution.

True science can have no fundamental conflict with the Christian faith. To try to avoid the claims of Christianity by saying that science has made it redundant or proved it false is to try to dodge the issue. No, science continues to explore the 'music' of the universe by examining the workings of melody, harmony, chord progressions and even the notes themselves. To discover its *composer* requires a completely different method of exploration – allowing the polyphony of sounds to touch you, tuning in to the overall theme and refining your ear to catch that unique sound which betrays his identity.

7

Isn't the church full of hypocrites?

I asked over 100 people from a wide variety of backgrounds and occupations who attend my church to list the reasons why they felt Christianity was unpopular with those they worked with. Many reasons were given, but the one that came up the most frequently was *the way Christians behaved*. The thrust of the argument was: 'Christianity is great! It is *Christians* who are a pain in the neck.'

Let's be honest and say that Christianity has its fair share of hypocrites. Every time we see headlines in the Sunday papers like 'Vice vicar in love nest scandal', or read of priests abusing children, or learn that a supposedly born-again Christian celebrity has divorced his wife or cheated the Inland Revenue, we begin to wonder if the whole thing isn't just a farce. Worse still, we may actually know someone in our street who claims to be a Christian but who is a bad neighbour and known in the area for being thoroughly disagreeable. Perhaps you work with a Christian who arrives late and leaves early, does a poor job of work and takes things home with him which don't belong to him. No wonder people say, 'If this is Christianity, I don't want anything to do with it!'

And if it is, I don't either! But is it? Are Christians just a bunch of people who talk big but live bad? Before we take a look at what lies behind all this supposed Christian hypocrisy, let's destroy a couple of assumptions.

First, sometimes people accuse the Church or individual Christians of hypocrisy, but fail to notice the same hypocrisy in themselves! Which of us can honestly claim to have never said something we didn't really mean? Or never done something we said we wouldn't? If a definition of hypocrisy is 'to say one thing and do another', then we are *all* hypocrites.

Unless we are honest enough to make this admission, the whole discussion that follows is pointless. When we diagnose hypocrisy as a Christian disease, it must be with the understanding that we are fellow sufferers! After all, it's only fair to give equal weight to the hypocrisy that Christians often see in people who are not Christians. Some will live all their lives with no time for God or his Church and then want a priest or minister to give them a Christian funeral, hedging their bets in case there was something in Christianity after all. Parents want their child christened but have no real intention of fulfilling the promises they make at baptism or of coming to church themselves. Young couples want to get married in church because it will look nice in the photos but make promises to a God they don't believe in, inside a building they don't intend to visit again. Sheer hypocrisy!

All this illustrates how hard it is for any of us to be truly blameless. Yes, some Christians are hypocrites, but the Church has not cornered the market in hypocrisy. We are *all* guilty.

Second, hypocrisy is often confused with deliberate manipulation. I suppose that the arena in which hypocrisy is most common is politics. The average person takes what politicians say in the run-up to an election with a pinch of salt. We assume they will promise almost anything to get elected and, once they are, will conveniently forget any policy too awkward to put into practice. Now, whether this is true of every politician or not, as a society we have tended to equate this deliberate distortion of what someone really thinks (in order to achieve the goal of election) with hypocrisy. 'He never really meant any of that stuff he said. He'd say anything to become an MP.' There are other examples of this kind of hypocrisy. There's the man who comes to your door offering to concrete your drive – then you never see him or your deposit again. There are people who sell phoney investment deals. There's the car salesman who assures you that 'this car has only had one careful owner'. There are always going to be people willing to lie deliberately to achieve their own ends.

However, this kind of hypocrisy (cynical manipulation) is very rare indeed among Christians. The cantankerous Christian boss or the vicar who ends up in bed with the choir mistress are more examples of human failure than of Christian hypocrisy. This does not excuse their behaviour – they claimed to live by a set of standards (the Christian faith) and did not. In this sense they *are* hypocrites. But they cannot be condemned with the same venom as those who manipulate others for their own selfish ends. Any reasonable person would want to condemn both kinds of hypocrisy, but the manipulator deserves our anger and the failure our pity.

Now let's tackle head-on this 'Christians are hypocrites' business. I am going to make what I believe are five factual statements to help us decide whether to accept or reject Christianity on the basis of the way some Christians behave.

1. 'Christian' does not always mean Christian!

The word 'Christian' is used in so many ways it is hard to know what it means. There are, for example, political parties called 'Christian Democrats', a fighting unit in the Middle East called the 'Christian Militia' and a church known to me where they have a Christian cabaret!

People who call themselves Christians may not actually *be* Christians and, if they are not, it would hardly be fair to judge real Christians by what these so-called Christians say or do. For example, one man in the last century stood for more elections than anyone else – Lord David Sutch, known as Screaming Lord Sutch, representing the Monster Raving Loony Party. His behaviour and speeches were colourful, to say the least! But if people started to draw the conclusion that *all* members of the aristocracy acted like this, a real lord would be quick to point out that Lord Sutch was no such thing!

So it is only fair to make a judgement on Christianity on the basis of how real Christians behave. Someone may go to church, be friendly and honest and believe in God, but still not be a Christian. The Bible is quite clear about real Christians. A Christian is someone who has a personal relationship with Jesus, an experience so profound that it is sometimes described as being born all over again. Many accusations of hypocrisy may be levelled at people who are Christians in name only, but not at those in whom the revolution of meeting Jesus has taken place.

Imagine how peeved you would be if you had worked for five years to gain a doctorate degree, and someone else had written to a Mickey Mouse University in America and got a doctorate in the same subject for ten dollars and the tops from three packets of cornflakes. Imagine how angry you would feel if it was assumed that you both had the same level of learning. Christians sometimes feel very much like this – frustrated at being judged on the basis of those who share their name but not the reality of their experience.

This information – that people who call themselves Christians may not necessarily be real Christians – can come as quite a shock if we have glibly assumed what people claimed about themselves was true. But should we be so surprised? Our society is expert at substituting perspex for glass, Quorn for meat, NutraSweet for sugar, and – more seriously – lust for love and charity for compassion. Only the discerning can tell they are being deceived. When confronted with hypocrisy, we must ask ourselves if the behaviour we are condemning has been committed by a *real* Christian or by an extremely plausible imitation of the real thing.

From time to time, violence at football matches becomes a serious issue. The football stands, once the scene of a good family afternoon out becomes a venue for the brave or reckless. Team managers speak out against the hooligan element masquerading as football supporters. The fact is that the troublemakers turn up at the ground, look like real supporters and sing the same songs – yet are condemned by everyone for not being *real* supporters. It would be strange logic to come to the conclusion that football was a bad game or that there were no genuine fans just because some people went to the ground to fight, not to watch football! It would be equally illogical to dismiss Christianity as a whole because some so-called Christians acted wrongly, or to condemn genuine fans of the Christian faith because of the actions of others who appear to be like them. These people may look like Christians, sing the same songs, even attend the same church. But only if they have had an encounter with Jesus are they really Christians.

Of course, we must be honest enough to admit that even real Christians can be hypocrites. When they are, then it is perfectly reasonable to question their sincerity and the validity of the Christian faith as a whole. However, when we do this, we come up against some other problems.

2. Some people who aren't Christians behave better than Christians!

True!

... if by this we mean that we know some non-Christians who are nicer, kinder and more helpful than some Christians. We may even feel that *we* are better people than some Christians we know. We could well be! Sometimes those arguing against the Christian faith take the next steps in the argument like this ...

> 'I'm not a hypocrite like Joe Christian. He takes things from work/beats his wife/tells lies, and I am far too honest to do that. My behaviour is better than his, so it's likely his Christianity isn't any good. It certainly doesn't help him much, so I don't see why I should need it either.'

On the face of it this sounds extremely reasonable. Criticising Joe involves two basic ideas: first, Joe's hypocrisy discredits his Christianity (see next section) and, second, the *difference* in *our* behaviour discredits his Christianity.

But wait a minute! Is it fair for us to compare ourselves with Joe in such a simplistic way? What if Joe is under massive pressure we know nothing about? Close to the poverty line? Near to a nervous breakdown? Looking after a terminally-ill child? None of this would excuse Joe's behaviour or make it right, but it might explain it.

Questions like these highlight the great difficulty in making judgements on other people's lives without knowing all the facts. What needs to be established is whether or not Joe is a better person now *than he would have been if he had not become a Christian*. For example, if Joe had been a psychopathic killer and now only takes paper-clips from work, I'd say a good case could be made for the effectiveness of his Christianity!

This leads us to clarify what Joe is claiming as a Christian. He is *not* claiming to be perfect; he is only claiming to be forgiven and in the process of improving! He is going to make mistakes and fall flat on his face. But because of God's power inside him, he is slowly becoming more like the Jesus he follows and less like the hypocritical Joe he was and sometimes still is.

Knowing where someone has come from does make a tremendous difference to the way we make judgements about them. At first sight, you would treat a 20-stone man recommending his diet to you as a bit of a joke. But if you found out he used to be 30 stone, you might think again even if you only weigh 12 stone. Some Christians are like this. They have got a long way to go but they are moving in the right direction.

Let's put the words into Joe's mouth:

> 'I know I sometimes do things that are wrong and which seem to go against my beliefs. I'm sorry and know I shouldn't do this, but I'm better than I was. I'm not trying to make excuses, but I took a step in the right direction when I became a Christian. I feel Jesus has forgiven me. I'm not perfect yet, but each day God is changing me into a new and better person. One day I'll be the man he wants me to be!'

So, just because my behaviour is better than Joe's doesn't discredit his Christianity. But this leads us on to another question and the third statement.

3. Hypocrisy doesn't discredit Christianity

It is perfectly reasonable to be annoyed by hypocrisy; but is it reasonable to then reject the faith which the hypocritical person holds?

One winter, during a particularly cold spell, I came downstairs to discover our pipes had frozen. After an initial dribble there was not a drop of water in the entire house. Eventually, after a day without water, the offending pipe was discovered and warmed up. I didn't realise how much water we used until the day we couldn't get any! All this was very frustrating, but can you imagine me saying, 'That's it, I'm disgusted! I don't want anything to do with water ever again. I'll wash with milk! I'll . . .

I'll . . . I'll never trust water again!' Anyone who reasons like this should expect a visit from the men in white coats! We all know that there is absolutely nothing wrong with the water, just a defect in the means of getting it to us.

In the same way, God has given his message to people (Christians) and has told them to pass it on to others. They often fail to pass it on – their lives get clogged up with all sorts of rubbish – and God's love has a hard time getting through to anyone else. However, to blame God for this, or to imagine that he has somehow been discredited, is as illogical as refusing to use the water. We cannot reasonably dismiss Christianity because some of the people through whom it passes are 'defective pipes'. Car breakdowns don't mean we never drive again. Power failures don't discredit electricity. If anyone doubted the existence or usefulness of electricity just because they have an old stereo that doesn't work, we would doubt their sanity. Yet so many people arrive at this conclusion about Christianity on the basis of 'power failure' among some Christians. There is absolutely nothing wrong with their power supply; they just seem to have faulty connections.

We ought not to leave this section without saying that although hypocrisy gives us no logical reason for rejecting Christianity, it does make us sceptical on emotional grounds. This is what makes hypocrisy so dangerous: we see it and instinctively feel something is wrong. It's a little like watching a bald man selling hair restorer: we sense an inconsistency and emotionally we reject the whole thing as fake. But what if the plain fact was that he enjoyed being bald or had not got round to using the restorer yet? The truth is his baldness tells us absolutely nothing about whether the hair restorer works or not; it only makes us feel uneasy with his claim. The only way to know for sure is to try it for ourselves and see. Inconsistent and hypocritical Christians do make it harder for others to believe that the Christian message works; but the only real test of Christianity's validity is for us to explore its claims for ourselves.

So far in this chapter we have tried to explain some of the things it is reasonable to say about Christians who are hypocrites. (And some of the things which it is not!) The next two sections look at some of the positive statements Christians can make about hypocrisy.

4. There are only fakes of valuable things

A hypocrite is a fake – someone who claims to be something different from what he is. But have you noticed that there are only fakes of things that are of value? Rembrandts are copied because the originals are so highly prized. No forger on earth would waste time trying to produce an exact copy of the doodles I draw when I'm on the phone! The originals just aren't worth anything! Yet any art gallery would confirm that the more famous the painter the more alert they have to be for forgeries. And so with Christianity. Anything that claims to be this wonderful is bound to suffer from imitations.

In both cases the issue is cost. If you really want a Picasso in your living room, you may settle for a reproduction because it's cheaper. Many people settle for something that looks like Christianity because they are not prepared to pay the cost involved in having the real thing. The presence of hypocrisy does seem to imply a genuinely valuable faith behind it. After all, you can't have a fake without an original. Ever seen a fake £11 note? Of course not! Because the real thing doesn't exist. If there are fake Rembrandts, there must be real ones. If there are fake fivers there must be real ones and, if there are fake Christians . . .

Hypocrisy certainly does discredit individual Christians, but it does seem to point beyond the individual to a valuable and genuine faith.

5. Jesus hates hypocrisy

It's important to finish this chapter by making clear that none of the arguments we have used in any way excuses hypocrisy in itself. All true Christians hate hypocrisy because *Jesus hated it.*

Let's not be in any doubt just how vigorously Christianity's founder opposed hypocrisy of every kind. Listen to these words from 'gentle Jesus meek and mild'. They are addressed to a group of religious leaders.

> You religious leaders are hypocrites! You pretend to be holy and you say long prayers in public; but behind the scenes you throw innocent widows out of their homes. You are sons of hell and anyone you convert becomes twice as bad as you under your influence. You are blind guides and fools; clean on the outside, dirty where it counts on the inside, hypocrites! You are greedy, extortionate, legalistic, deceitful . . . more like snakes than the shepherds you are supposed to be! (From Matthew chapter 23.)

Talk about angry – we are talking volcanic! Anything that smacks of double standards is exposed for what it is by Jesus. He hated hypocrisy then and he hates it now. Anyone who is against hypocrisy has an ally in Jesus of Nazareth. The good news for all of us is that, while he hates hypocrisy, he can still find it in his heart to love hypocrites.

8

God, people and Christians – FAQs

Q: How can a God of love send people to hell?

Hell means total separation from everything good. The flames described in the Bible may be picture language, but the reality they represent is no figment of the imagination. One of the reasons hell exists is because of the seriousness with which God takes the decisions of men and women. If we choose to reject him, his offer of life and way of escape from all the dirtiness in the world, he refuses to overrule our decision. He won't force us to accept his love – this would rob us of the privilege of choice and make us mere androids. So we have to take the consequences of our decisions. This means that, by choosing to live without God, we have indeed *chosen to live without God, now and for ever.*

It is no use asking why we can't opt to live *without* God in this life and to live *with* him in the next. The question completely misses the point about the radical nature of our choice. For example, suppose we choose not to have any children of our own and then, at the age of 80, change our minds and want to have grown-up children around to look after us. By then it's too late. Our earlier decision had inevitable consequences. So it is with our decision about God. There comes a point (death) when our earlier decision is too far gone to change, which means we have chosen to spend eternity living in the presence of our own sinfulness and in the absence of God.

All this shows that, far from God sending people to hell, they

seem to be sending themselves. After all, it would be unreasonable to blame the doctor for my ill health if I refuse to take the
medicine he prescribed! The divine doctor has diagnosed the
sin-sickness of mankind and offered a forgiveness-cure. If we
refuse or ignore the offer, we will have to live with the disease.
This is what hell is – living after death with all our worst traits
still raging inside us, only now they are unrestrained by God or
social convention, a seething mass of unforgiven vices and unre-
solved conflicts. God does not want *anyone* to go to hell (see 1
Timothy 2:4), so he has prepared a way for the human race to
escape its horrors. He is in the business of getting people into
heaven, not sending them to hell!

Q: Isn't Christianity just a psychological crutch?

No!

. . . not if you mean that the faith a Christian has is just wishful
thinking, all in the mind. As if we can dismiss someone's faith
by implying that in some way he or she *needs* to believe it and
therefore does. This is patronising for a start and a very dangerous argument indeed – for the person who uses it! Take a
double-edged knife, place your thumb over one of the sharp
edges and put the other on a piece of wood. As you push hard
the wood is cut. So is your thumb! The knife, like the argument
above, cuts both ways. After all, a Christian could also retort that
an atheist is someone who doesn't want to bother about obeying
God's commands, so – hey presto! – there is no God! But this
kind of atheism is equally 'all in the mind'.

No!

. . . not if you mean Christian experience is *just* psychological. It
does, of course, involve psychological aspects of our lives – our
minds, emotions and wills. But this is not the whole story. For
example, a scientist could describe cricket in terms of velocity,

mass, density and distance. He could be exhaustive in defining every principle involved. Still, he could not say that cricket is just a series of principles in physics! There are other dimensions – the rules of the game, winning and competing, and so on. Christian conversion is like this. It is psychological, but when you have said this you have only commented on one small aspect of the whole experience.

No!

... not if you mean Christianity is a crutch like alcohol or drugs, something to help the weak through tough situations – as if Christians were basically failures as people and needed something to help them get by. 'Is Christianity *true?*' is the vital question. American writer and speaker Joni Eareckson-Tada became a quadriplegic after a diving accident when she was 17; yet she has said, 'I believe in Jesus not because it is easy but because it is true.' If Christianity was false, it would be a useless crutch. At least alcohol works, even if only for a short time.

But if Christianity *is* true, it is a cure not a crutch.

Yes!

... if you mean Christianity helps people to cope in tough times and overcome their difficulties.

Yes!

... if you mean Christianity is a source of strength and comfort to thousands.

Yes!

... if you mean Christianity provides a rock of unchanging certainty in an ever-changing world!

Q: Aren't Christians narrow-minded?

Yes!

... it has to be admitted that some Christians are locked into a series of petty rules and regulations which have more to do with tradition than the teaching of Jesus. But if by the question you mean that some Christian teaching seems narrow and restrictive – for example 'Sex outside marriage is wrong' – then a couple of things need to be said.

First, these seeming restrictions aren't half as narrow from the inside as they appear from the outside. When I first went to the House of Commons, I was shown round to what appeared to be a side entrance. This door was so narrow that you had to enter in single file. It was so unimposing! Do our MPs really meet in a poky old house? Once you get in, the change is remarkable. Majestic archways, huge halls and miles of corridors. From the outside, small and unimpressive. From the inside, huge and spacious. A bit like Dr Who's Tardis! Similarly, when we become Christians, the teaching that looked so restrictive is in fact quite the opposite.

Christians don't feel restricted by the Bible's teaching about sex – its very narrowness gives real security to marriage and the freedom to develop a meaningful sex life with a permanent partner you can trust. When you contrast this with the broad teaching of our permissive society, we are beginning to discover that this 'freedom' means a freedom to break up someone else's marriage, cheapen relationships, hurt other members of the family, bring up a child alone ... The list of hurts this freedom has caused could go on and on. Not to mention the freedom to get AIDS or a whole range of sexually transmitted diseases. Compared with all this, Christianity's 'narrowness' seems a pretty good deal!

Second, sometimes 'narrow-mindedness' is just wisdom wearing a different hat. Why don't we stop being so narrow-minded about our driving habits? 'How dare they restrict our freedom like this! I want to ... drive on any side of the road I like/

stop on green/ go on red/ use the north-bound carriageway when I next go south on the motorway. This is my right!' Of course, if you choose to exercise your right you will soon be dead right! Though we may resent them at times, we all know that these rules are for our own safety and the safety of fellow-travellers. Christians see God's rules in the same way: they are there for our protection and best interests, not to cramp our style.

Q: What about people who haven't heard about Jesus?

It really does seem unfair that God should judge people when they haven't had the chance to hear about Jesus.

Well, let's get one thing clear from the start – God *is* going to act fairly. That is his nature – just, fair and compassionate. This much is guaranteed: when every human being comes face to face with their Creator, no one will be able to complain that they got a raw deal.

God has given two clues about himself to every person on earth. The first is the world about us – its beauty, order and design. Live in my house while I am away, and my books, CDs and the state of my garden will tell you a great deal about me even though we may never have met. Live in God's world and the discerning person will notice the marks of his ownership every-where. The second clue is the conscience in all of us, that inner voice which keeps us uncomfortable when we do what we know to be wrong. It points out that we can't even live up to our own standards. It's a constant reminder, put there by God, that we need help to become the people we would like to be.

Unfortunately, nobody has ever lived up to their own stan-dards, let alone God's, so Jesus came to give us new power to do the right thing. There is no way to get this power except through his death and resurrection. However, this does not necessarily mean that an individual must be aware of Jesus' action on his or her behalf in order to receive its benefit.

When slavery was abolished in the British empire in 1833, thousands of people in Africa were made safe from the threat of captivity and abduction to the West Indies and the Americas. Many of them knew nothing about the British Government and even less about the act of Parliament which guaranteed their freedom! Despite this ignorance, they enjoyed the freedom the act obtained for them. In the same way, any person anywhere who is really sorry for the wrong in their lives and throws themself completely on God's mercy for their salvation can enjoy the benefits of the Christian message, even though they do not know the facts about Jesus' death and resurrection.

Q: What about people who are unable to hear about Jesus?

This question is similar to the last. Usually people want to include in this question two different groups: those who were born before Jesus came, and those who do not have the capacity to understand the Christian message, such as children who die in infancy or people with learning difficulties.

First, throughout the Bible, the way to God is the same – *by faith in God's mercy* – and not, even in the Old Testament, by keeping the commandments. All the ancient heroes of the Bible who are said to have pleased God did so by faith. He accepted their faith on the basis of what Jesus was *going* to do. They enjoyed the benefits of Jesus' death and resurrection even though it had not yet happened. I may, for example, get my wife a gift on the strength of a pay rise I have been promised. She experiences the benefit of the increase before I get the money because I know it is coming! Similarly, God chose to accept people in Old Testament times on the strength of what he knew was coming, in response to their faith.

Second, people who don't have the ability to understand the Christian message will not be judged as if they did! God is perfectly fair and understands their limitations better than we do: they will not be automatically damned because of their inability to grasp his message. The Bible does, however, indicate clearly the people who *are* going to be judged – those who reject the message, and those who hear it but never get round to making a decision about it! If you are reading this book, you have the capacity to understand the facts about Jesus Christ. Very young babies and people with terribly damaged minds would seem incapable of either the rejection or the delaying tactics the Bible so strongly condemns.

God does not want *anyone* to be lost, and he is deeply concerned about every human being. When he expresses special concern for the weak and defenceless in society, we can be certain that he has tragic circumstances, like the death of a baby, near to his heart. We know he will do the just and fair thing.

Q: What about all these denominations?

The implication behind this question is usually that there are so many different ones to choose from, how can we possibly know which is right? Why don't all Christians believe the same things?

Well, firstly the differences between denominations are not as fundamental as some people think. The difference between Buddhism and Christianity is like the difference between chalk and cheese. In comparison, the difference between Baptist and Methodist is like that between Cheddar and Edam. Whatever the denomination, all true believers have a fundamental unity with all other true believers. This means that they are Christians first and Anglicans or Baptists, for example, second. The absolutely crucial questions have nothing to do with which denomination you belong to.

The most obvious differences are to do with the form the Sunday service takes. Some services are very quiet, others are noisy. Some follow a set pattern, others never do the same thing two weeks running. Some ministers wear robes, some a suit, others jeans! But behind all these differences lie other, more complex areas of disagreement. Sometimes it is a matter of giving one of the truths in the Bible a special emphasis; or it may be a sincere disagreement about what the Bible actually means. Occasionally, it is an accident of history, where a personal squabble between two leaders hardened over the years into rival groupings. Whatever the reasons, we can't escape the fact that there are more denominations around than ever before.

But we must not make the mistake of rejecting Christianity because there are so many churches to choose from. This would be as absurd as giving up food because we were bewildered by the variety of supermarkets. Let's make two observations for the discerning church 'shopper'.

First, all true Christians agree on the fundamentals of the faith. So much so that they could happily meet in one another's homes and talk about Jesus without the question of denomination ever arising. Even if there were a million denominations, nothing could alter the basis of their faith – Jesus Christ.

Second, there are 'dead' churches in every denomination. So don't choose a local church just because it is linked with a denomination you like. Check a few out and go to one where they talk about Jesus, believe in the Bible and you sense something special during the service. And, by the way, there won't be any denominations in heaven, so don't worry about them too much in this life!

Q: Can you prove that Christianity is true?

This depends on the kind of proof you are looking for. The Christian faith can't be examined in a laboratory. But then, all the really important things are like this. Love, peace, friendship, fun – none of these can be placed under a microscope. In fact, we accept the vast majority of things in our lives without any strictly scientific proof.

There is, however, another kind of proof which we use all the time, almost without thinking about it. We sometimes call this 'legal' proof and it rests on two levels of enquiry – eyewitness accounts and supporting evidence. If I wanted to prove where I went on holiday, I would produce supporting evidence like my passport with a country's stamp in it, my photos and the bill for the hotel room. In addition, I would talk about an overgrown cliff walk, an unbelievably grubby corner cafe and a newly

painted pier – all this indicating that I had actually seen the place with my own eyes. Christianity is open to *this* kind of proof. I will have to conduct my own defence and it goes something like this:

I have examined as much of the supporting evidence that I could lay my hands on, the main document being the Bible. I have found it to be thoroughly reliable. I have had the experience that the Bible describes and I can now talk about things in a way which would simply be impossible if I had not seen this truth for myself. On the basis of the supporting evidence (the Bible and the experience of others) and what I have experienced personally, I have come to the conclusion that Christianity is true.

We can prove Christianity for ourselves by the same method. Examine the supporting evidence as honestly as possible. Then be prepared to accept God's offer. When you do, something happens that opens your eyes to a whole new world – a marvellous, exciting (and demanding!) world filled with new things from horizon to horizon. Enjoy the view.

But please note – collecting 'legal' proof takes time. You are not going to prove or disprove Christianity in ten minutes. Such a crucial issue deserves careful and thoughtful enquiry.

Q: Isn't the Church out of date and out of touch?

Sometimes a trip to church can be like experiencing a time warp. You might find yourself back in the last century, or even the one before. To boldly go where no man would want to bother going! You could be forgiven for thinking that you had wandered into a museum by mistake. Once the service begins, you may be attacked by 'Thees' and 'Thous', confused by instructions to 'approach the Throne of Grace' (whoever she is!) and asked to sing about the 'waste places of Jerusalem breaking forth with joy'. No wonder it all seems out of date and irrelevant.

Wait a minute though! Lots of churches are *not* like this any more. Some big changes have happened in the last few years. If you last went as a child, some of the churches in your area could be a hundred times more up-to-date than you remember. There are churches that meet in people's homes, in community halls and even in pubs! You might well understand and relate to more than you think.

Talking of understanding, Christians do have their own special vocabulary. I used to think that chips had something to do with fish, a byte was what you got from a mosquito and software was an old woolly jumper! Now I know this is computer talk, a specialised language to explain a specific activity. In Christianity we have words like 'faith' and 'salvation' which we cannot do without. These words are not old-fashioned; they are just part of the technical language of the Christian faith. Once you get the hang of the terms, things become much clearer.

The other thing to remember is this: just because something is old doesn't necessarily mean it is old-fashioned. Breathing and eating have been around since the creation of man and few of us are going to stop doing either merely because they have been happening a long time. In fact, in some ways, the reverse is true. Haven't all things of real value been around for aeons – love, peace, friendship? Christianity is old in the sense that its values are permanent. Most of us would rather base our lives on this than on some trendy new idea which will be out of date in months.

9

Christianity and my life – FAQs

Q: Can't I live a good life without being a Christian?

Yes!

. . . if you mean 'Can people who are not Christians do kind and helpful things for others?' Many people with no Christian faith at all work for charities, give time and money to needy causes and are good neighbours. You don't need to be a Christian to help an old lady across the road.

No!

. . . not if you mean 'Can I be as good as it is possible for me to be, without being a Christian?' However good any of us are, none of us would claim to be perfect, so there is always room for improvement. Jesus Christ offers an inner strength to make us better people. If we want to be good people, why on earth would we turn down his offer of help? Even if you are very good indeed, there is no area which would not be improved by knowing and following Jesus.

No!

. . . not if you mean 'Am I good enough for God?'. However good we may be, we cannot meet God's 'goodness standard'. Let's imagine a competition to jump across the English Channel. The first competitor, a 70-year-old alcoholic, manages three feet. His rival, a 20-year-old decathlon champion, manages 25 feet; he is vastly superior to his fellow competitor. But this difference pales into insignificance compared with the 22 miles they would need to jump to get all the way across! God's 'goodness standard' is Jesus Christ. Compared with him the very best of us fails abysmally. And, of course, the very worst fail too.

Good *and* bad people need Jesus. Good people may feel they need him a little less, but they do need him just the same. The difference between good and bad people could be measured in 'feet'; the difference between good people and Jesus could be measured in 'miles'! There is no point in claiming to be 'as good as the next man' or 'better than those people from the church', or to say you 'wouldn't harm a soul' – even if every word of it is true. There was a rich young ruler in the Bible who could say all those things and he still went away from Jesus a sad and unfulfilled man. (Check out the story in Luke 18:18–24).

It's right to do good deeds. Our world needs more people who give selflessly of their time and money to help others. But if we are counting on our goodness to earn God's approval, we are in for a nasty shock. No one is good enough.

Q: Can't I be a Christian without going to church?

Well, yes, it is possible. It would be a mistake to think that *the only thing* you need to do to be a Christian is to go to church. Christians should be fully involved in every aspect of life, working to change things for the better, to care for the poor, to visit the sick, and generally to show God's love to the world. Christianity is not a Sunday-only activity!

But it would also be a mistake to think that this means you need never set foot in a church. You might survive on chocolate cake and lemonade, make love in a bed of nettles or sun-bathe in the Antarctic! These activities are all possible, but no one would view them as being the best options available! Similarly, we have to say that the best option for a Christian is to be part of a local church. Why?

Because real Christians need to

Before you become a Christian, going to church regularly seems a pretty stiff requirement. When you are a Christian, you soon see the immense value of being with other Christians – to learn together and to encourage one another. Without this kind of support our faith would struggle to survive, indeed it would be questionable whether we were real Christians at all. Footballers need a team; however much they practise on their own, even if they can balance the ball on their noses or kick it into a net half a mile away, they still need a team to be real footballers. Football is a team game. So is Christianity.

Because real Christians want to

It's very hard to describe, but nothing on earth can replace the sense of God's presence when Christians get together for worship. Of course, some moments in church are better than others, but there is always the potential for another encounter with God. Something inside us urges us to be with God's people.

Because real Christians want the best

The original question seems to imply 'Can I get away with not going to church?' Yes, is the answer. But is it the best thing for a Christian? How much can you take out of a car before it stops being a car? Radio, seat covers and ashtray? No problem. Horn, indicators and headlights? Possibly. Brakes, tyres and engine? At some point it ceases to be a car. But long before getting to that point it ceases to be a very good car. There are lots of things you can get away without doing as a Christian, but sooner or later you reach the point where you cannot be one at all. And, long before you reach that point you have ceased to be a very good Christian. Why settle for mediocrity? Why not go for the best? As a Christian this will mean regular church attendance.

Q: Won't becoming a Christian make me boring?

I have heard people talk about their decision to become
Christians as if this involved a change from an exciting life to
one which has all the thrills of watching paint dry! 'I used to go
to parties every night, had loads of girls/guys, life was a blast.
Then (adopting serious tone and expression) I became a
Christian. Now I don't do any of the stuff I used to do. I go to
prayer meetings, read my Bible and help to make the coffee after
the service.' Certainly sounds dull! But wait a minute . . .

Being a Christian is about following Jesus and becoming like
him. There is no way Jesus could be described as boring. He gave
up the security of a nine-to-five job as a carpenter at the age of
30, gathered a mixed bunch of characters around him, and set
off on a three-year walk round Galilee and Judea. He was regularly misunderstood, often went without a bed for the night,
was eventually betrayed by one of his closest followers and suffered a bloody and cruel death. During his life he became
known for practising medicine without a licence, drawing large
crowds, doing amazing things with fish and bread, and making
outrageous statements about following him and living for ever!
Jesus is anything *but* boring, and his followers are offered the
same new dimension of living. Some Christians lock this new
life up tight within them and miss some of its exciting dimensions. But if we let this Jesus-life have full sway, our lives need
never be dull.

The other important thing to remember when you see
Christians doing things which seem dull and uninteresting
compared with your current lifestyle, is this: when you become
a Christian, the kind of things you enjoy doing changes. When I
was a child, my dad would cross his legs, sit me on his foot and
bounce me up and down. I wanted to do this again and again. It
was great! It will come as no surprise to you that I haven't
wanted to do this for years – nor, for that matter, has my father!
I now enjoy other things. When you become a Christian, some
of the things you used to do seem unattractive, even boring, in
comparison with what you have available to you now.

Q: I'm happy as I am – why should I change?

'Things are going well for me, thank you. I have my little ups and downs, but basically life is fine just the way it is. Why should I change what I believe?'

Sometimes we do arrive at a settled lifestyle – no money worries, a comfortable home and a secure job. In situations like this, Christianity seems irrelevant at best and interfering at worst.

However, while *you* may be happy as you are, others may not be so sure. Your spouse may want to see change in you, and so might your boss or workmates. Ask your children or your parents if they are happy with the way you are. Saying 'I really don't need to change' could just be the selfish assertion, 'Blow you, Jack, I'm all right!' – in which case you most certainly do need to change!

Let's, for argument's sake, say that you *are* happy as you are and those around you seem to agree. Could it be that your satisfaction with yourself is based on an inadequate view of happiness? I mean, if you only ever had dry bread, you would not be able to imagine the delights of Belgian chocolates or strawberries and cream! Christians maintain that once you have discovered Christianity, everything else is like dry bread! So to say that you are happy as you are is to rob yourself of whole new vistas of fulfilment. Jesus said that he had come to bring a new, richer quality of life. He keeps his promise.

Could it also be that your happiness is based on ignorance of the real situation? What if you knew that, at this moment of happiness, the first cancerous cell had appeared in your body? You would change your eating habits, take medication or do anything else the doctor suggested. You would be stupid to say that you were not going to change your lifestyle because you felt happy. Sin, the Bible says, is an even more deadly disease which affects all of us. It is silently growing away inside us and, if it continues, will prove eternally fatal. No wonder Christians think that a happiness which has not come to terms with this problem is very superficial. After all, an ostrich with its head in the sand may be happy. But is it safe?

Q: How can one man's death so long ago possibly affect me?

Some people are unable to see how a man killed nearly 2000 years ago could possibly have any relevance for them today. The death of a Judean carpenter in some obscure corner of the world hardly seems likely to make a primetime TV news bulletin, never mind be anything to do with me hundreds of years later.

On 28 June 1914, an Austrian archduke was killed by a Serbian nationalist. His tragic death was reported but its significance completely overlooked. Within six weeks it became clear that this incident was the fuse which triggered off World War One! Millions were killed or horribly injured and the map of Europe was decisively altered. The whole history of the world was changed by that assassination in Sarajevo. In a much more profound way, the death of Jesus has affected all of us. The presence of the Church, the Bible, our calendar, and much more, highlights the impact he made. Billions remember his death every Easter and millions of those claim that his death has changed them personally. But how? For Christians, Jesus is not just a dead hero but a living Saviour.

Some years ago a plane crashed into an ice-cold river. Television cameras recorded the heroic attempts of one man to help with the rescue by plunging into the river to drag survivors from the wreckage. After one person had been pulled to safety he returned for another. He never came back to the shore. For thousands watching on television that man was a hero, but for the person he rescued he was much, much more. He was a saviour. The same is true about every Christian's attitude to Jesus. He gave his life so that we could live. Because of the wrong we do, we deserve to be punished. But, instead, Jesus took that punishment for us so we don't need to be punished after all. No wonder Christians are grateful to Jesus for dying to save us.

Q: It may be right for you – but why should that mean it's right for me?

Thousands of Christians have had this said to them and it usually puts a stop to any further discussion about faith in Jesus. But it shouldn't. It is yet another of those statements which sound sensible but actually hold as much water as a sieve. Let's have a look at three of the holes.

It's illogical

If Christianity is wrong, then it's wrong for all of us. The Christian faith makes major demands. If it is wrong, I am wasting lots of valuable time at church and Christian events, being cheated out of a sizeable proportion of my income and generally throwing my life away on a worthless cause. What kind of friend are you, saying it's OK if I believe all this nonsense?

And if Christianity is true, the statement is equally illogical. People often talk about it as if they were comparing cars. 'I know you're really keen on your Jaguar but I'm perfectly happy with my Ford.' Behind this attitude lies a complete misunderstanding about the nature of Christianity. Christianity is either true or false. This means it is either true for both of us or for neither of us. We can illustrate the logical absurdity of this statement by making the subject of the statement 'America': 'It's OK for you to believe in America, but it's not for me.' America is either a place on Planet Earth or it isn't. Whether you believe it or not won't change the facts! One of us is wrong.

It's dangerous

Christianity is basically a rescue operation. It claims to have diagnosed mankind's basic disease (sin) and is offering a course of treatment for its cure. Millions are taking the medicine, which sometimes takes a while to work and the improvement is not always spectacular. But are you really in a position to think of yourself as a special case? 'The cure is OK for you, but I'd rather not bother with it' hardly sounds a safe and sensible response.

It's silly!

The Christian faith offers joy and peace. Are you seriously saying it's OK for me to have this but you don't want it? It offers a relationship with God, eternal joy and a unique quality of life here on earth. You don't want a good time when you die? Or even right now?

If you think Christianity is *wrong*, say so! But if you *really* think it's all right for me, you should at least take the time to consider whether it might be all right for you too. To reject it without doing so is surely to be somewhat perverse!

But I'm already a Christian!

If you really are a Christian, that's great. But how do you *know* you are a Christian? What is it that makes you think you are?

Here are a few of the most common reasons people give to support their claim to be a Christian.

'I go to church'

Many people go to church to worship God; but many others go out of habit, to be seen by the right people or to please the wife/husband! Lots of young people go because they can't get out of it.

But going to a sports centre doesn't make you an athlete. You have to get changed and get involved in training or working out. Going to church doesn't make you a Christian. You have to be changed and start to behave like one.

'I was born a Christian ...

... in a Christian country' the argument usually continues. Sorry, being born in a garage wouldn't make you a car! No one is born a Christian any more than anyone is born with pierced ears. Both things involve a definite decision on our part.

'I believe in God'

So does the devil, and it would be difficult to describe him as Christian! So do thousands of Muslims, and they would never dream of describing themselves as Christians.

There are lots of other reasons people give: 'I pray', 'I give money to charity', 'I'm basically a nice person', and so on and so on. At the heart of the problem is confusion about what a Christian really is. Your definition may be just as good as mine. Compared with God's definition, none of our own matter too much. So what does the Bible say?

Real Christians . . .

- recognise they need help – *All of us have sinned and fallen short of God's glory* (Romans 3:23).
- are ready to turn their backs on everything they know to be wrong – *'Turn back to God! Be baptised in the name of Jesus Christ, so that your sins will be forgiven . . .'* (Acts 2:38).
- trust Jesus to put things right – *Christ carried the burden of our sins. He was nailed to the cross, so that we would stop sinning and start living right* (1 Peter 2:24).
- invite Jesus to be in charge of their lives – *. . . some people accepted him and put their faith in him. So he gave them the right to be the children of God* (John 1:12).

Of course, there are many more things involved in living the Christian life, but these steps summarise the way to become one.

So, are you really a Christian?

10

Does it make sense?

If we're honest, we don't always find it easy to make sense of our lives. What are we here for, and why? What's the point of it all? Why can't we sort out the mess the world is in? The human race seems to stagger from one crisis to the next, and a lasting solution is as elusive as the pot of gold at the end of the rainbow. In theory, we all ought to be able to live together in harmony, but in practice we don't.

The confusion on our planet reminds me of Lewis Carroll's mock poem, 'Jabberwocky':

'Twas brillig, and the slithy toves
Did gyre and gimble in the wabe;
All mimsy were the borogoves,
And the mome raths outgrabe.

That's how the first verse goes. It rhymes, flows well and sounds impressive. But it's nonsense; the words don't mean anything. Many of our individual lives are like this. Superficially, everything in the garden is rosy, but closer examination reveals huge marshes of meaninglessness, clumps of contradiction and overgrowths of the weed 'confusion'.

Very few people are prepared to be as brutally honest as this when looking at their lives. But we need to be honest if we want to discover the truth about ourselves, as individuals and as a world. This really is the crunch for all thinking people: are we prepared to weigh all the evidence honestly and follow the facts we discover – wherever they lead?

Let's summarise the situation so far. All the previous chapters in this book have dealt with specific arguments often used to attack Christianity. I hope, even if you don't agree with all my answers, that you can see that Christians do have logical, reasonable grounds for their beliefs. It isn't just some wild, irrational leap of faith.

In fact, the Christian faith not only gives answers to questions about God; it also provides a sensible, cohesive explanation of why things are as they are in our world. C S Lewis explained his faith by saying that he believed in Christianity in the same way that he believed in the sun – not only because he could see it, but also because he could see everything else by its light. He was a Christian not simply because it seemed true in itself, but also because all other issues in life made more sense in the light of its teaching. Generations of Christians have found this to be true. Let's look at three issues which affect us all, and see what a Christian makes of them.

1. Right and wrong

Inside all of us is a sense that some things are right and some are wrong – but how did we get this sense? Christians say that since God made us in his image it's not surprising that we reflect his values. It's as if there were a small deposit of God within us that acts like an inner compass – one direction is right, the opposite is wrong. God put this compass there to give us an inner guide on how to behave. If we don't want to accept this explanation, what are the alternatives?

Some say that right and wrong are decided by the society we live in. They argue, for example, that in Britain it's perfectly all right to eat pork, but a Muslim or Jewish society would think this was very wrong. However, this argument fails to take into account the *basic* agreement between right and wrong that cuts across cultural boundaries. Of course *customs* vary from place to place and from generation to generation, but man's basic concept of right and wrong has been remarkably consistent. There is an amazing agreement, for example, that it is right to tell the truth and wrong to kill someone for the fun of it. And that kind of consensus has characterised the human race over thousands of years and across hundreds of countries.

Some say that 'right' and 'wrong' are only words to describe what is good for society as a whole, and society has evolved these values over the years for its own preservation. There is, however, no historical evidence for this evolution and, what's more, we can ask, 'Why should society be preserved?' There are a number of reasons but they all come round to the conclusion that 'It is right for human life to continue'. But *who* says that this is right? We just know it is. So we are back to our inner knowledge of right and wrong.

We don't leave it up to individuals to decide what is right and wrong, as though 'my view of right and wrong is just as good as yours' – for two reasons. First, it would result in chaos. If you made up your mind to believe that it was right to make love to your neighbour's wife whenever you wanted to, drown his dog if you felt like it, and break his children's legs for reclaiming the ball they had kicked into your garden, he may well feel that it was right to respond by shooting you in the head! No, if we all made up what was right and wrong as we went along, society would disintegrate in a matter of days.

And second, we know we would never accept this principle in practice: it just wouldn't work. Suppose that, in an argument with someone, you accused them of lying to you. They could put up a variety of defences – you misunderstood, circumstances have changed, you lied as well, and so on. But no one ever says, 'Of course I lied', holding the assumption that this is quite acceptable. We may have double standards, we may lie all the time, but we still *expect others* to tell the truth. People agree that this standard is right – lying is wrong. Without this agreement, no meaningful conversation is possible. We would never be able to trust anyone. So we live all the time in the knowledge that a real difference exists between right and wrong, and we are not free to change the rules whenever we want to. If God didn't put this knowledge there, then who or what did?

2. Problems in the world

There is all the difference in the world between *knowing* what is right and *doing* it. And not many people seem to be doing it! Daily the television brings news of the massive problems in the world – war, famine, terrorism, environmental destruction and civil unrest. Even in wealthy countries, unemployment and poverty cause deprivation and despair, especially in urban areas which are fast becoming concrete wildernesses of hopelessness and frustration.

What about the problems of family life? In the UK, recent statistics recorded a decline in divorce. So is this good news? Apparently not. Divorce rates are falling because marriage rates are falling. The numbers of people getting married fell by a quarter in the last decade of the twentieth century. And cohabitation is on the increase. Statistics for the opening years of the twenty first century show that three in 10 men and over a quarter of women cohabit before their first marriage.

Worldwide, child abuse is more widespread than we dreamed possible, and thousands of people live in daily fear of physical and verbal violence.

In the affluent West the suicide rate is rising, particularly among young men. In 2002 the UK government launched an initiative to curb this disturbing trend. Some 5000 people commit suicide in the UK every year, half of whom have had no contact with psychiatric health services. A survey revealed that one in six adults have seriously contemplated suicide at some point.

There has been a vast increase in stress-related illnesses. New diseases are emerging, and concern is growing about new debilitating allergies and falling fertility rates.

And that's just the tip of the iceberg. The catalogue of problems shows what a fine mess we have got ourselves into. What can be done? Many political solutions have been tried. The Old Mother Hubbards of national leadership search the political cupboard for answers in vain – it's empty. Down the centuries, monarchies and republics, democracies and dictatorships – and everything in between – have failed to produce truly just and fair societies. Economics, education, coercion and religion have all been explored in the search for some kind of answer. So far, it's a pretty depressing story. The UN says that 17 million children die of starvation around the world every year. At a conservative estimate, three times that number are aborted. We spend huge sums on arms, while for the lack of relatively small amounts people die from measles or the lack of clean water or go blind from cataracts.

What can be done? Picture a pig in a pigsty. Like most pigs, its manners leave a great deal to be desired. All that snorting, slobbering over food and enjoyment of mud-rolling. What can we do to change things? Well, we could burn the sty down and give the pig an antiseptic new home – which it probably wouldn't like! We could even give it such a luxurious pad that it would think it had died and gone to pig-heaven. Or we could tell the pig that if it didn't mend its ways we would start killing other pigs. Then again, we could send the pig on a self-help course to improve its attitudes, or provide it with a private tutor to educate it and then give it the right to vote. All this might help to make the pig affluent, clever and politically aware, and give it bags of self-confidence! But it is still a pig. A real pig. A pig with all its old habits and as strong a desire as ever to roll in the mud.

Christians argue that this is precisely why all the usual answers to the human condition fail: they do nothing to change the basic nature of people. They merely change our social and physical environment. People have got an inbuilt bias towards wrong. We know what the right thing to do is, but seem to have great difficulty doing it. The apostle Paul put it like this: 'I don't understand why I act the way I do. I don't do what I know is right. I do the things I hate . . . I know that my selfish desires won't let me do anything that is good. Even when I want to do right, I cannot' (Romans 7:15,18).

Jesus died to cancel out this bias towards wrong. And all true Christians, while still having the bias within them, have a new power in their lives to correct it. Just as a brace controls crooked teeth by pulling against their natural direction, so when Jesus comes into our lives he acts as a brace bringing our crooked behaviour back into line. Slowly but surely, he brings our actions into agreement with what he wants. The Christian solution, therefore, involves changes in our nature – deep changes that are sometimes described as being 'born again'. This takes very seriously indeed our contribution to the trouble in the world, arguing that unless people are changed the world never will be. Only a solution this radical will do. Everything else just scratches the surface.

The Jesus solution has implications for the world as a whole. Gordon Bailey's poem, 'Match of the Day' illustrates this:

> Mankind is but a football in a game that's played by fools,
> With no effective referee to emphasise the rules.
> Yet nailed upon a crossbar is a man, born for the role
> Whom stupid men have put to death, refusing his control.
> So as a consequence one finds an anarchistic game,
> Where death's a commonplace affair, and no one takes the blame.
> Within the sunlit stadium, mankind gets kicked around
> His hopes and dreams, and high ideals, lie lifeless on the ground.
> One commentator claims there isn't very long to play,
> That most of those involved will be sent off on Final Day.
> A starry universe spectates, and wonders at a sport,
> Where man must fill his pen with blood, to write the match report!

Alexander Solzhenitsyn has repeatedly affirmed that he believes only Christianity is a radical enough moral force to bring sanity back to his country, Russia, and to the world. Communism has failed but the present ruling government in Russia seems to have done no better.

But, to bring it right back to us as individuals, I have seen with my own eyes the revolutionary change brought about by knowing Jesus. Alcoholics, convicts, murderers and drug addicts

– all completely different after an encounter with Jesus. Hundreds of ordinary men and women too, in whom the change is less dramatic but no less real. Christianity provides the only powerful solution to the needs of individuals and the planet as a whole.

3. Life, the universe and everything

Here I am on Spaceship Earth, spinning round at thousands of miles per hour and still managing to keep my breakfast down! What am I doing here on this small planet as it whirls through vast stretches of space? Why was I born? Where am I going to end up? We can't live without some kind of answer to these questions, although thousands of the human race try to. They keep themselves busy with other things or push these thoughts to the backs of their minds for another day. But, like verbal boomerangs, the questions keep coming back, demanding answers.

The answers boil down to a choice between two stark alternatives. Either we're here for a purpose, or we aren't. We could be a great cosmic accident; a chance result of a haphazard evolutionary process begun at some point back in the mists of time; our presence on earth at the start of the third millennium the product of a chain of coincidences; our size, sex and personality the result of random combinations of genes; our existence one gigantic fluke.

In recent years, some scientists and philosophers *have* come to this conclusion. However, many of them discovered that it is virtually impossible to live consistently with this idea. They end up by believing one thing in theory, while actually living as if the opposite were true. And no wonder, when you consider the mind-blowing implications of this theory. If I, and everything about me, is here by accident, a number of things follow. Presumably, if my brain is the end product of random process, then the thoughts that come from it must ultimately have no significance. Words like 'sense' and 'nonsense' lose their meaning; they are only chemical impulses after all. Put simply,

A COSMIC ACCIDENT

any theory that says mankind is an outcome of chance has got an inbuilt destruct mechanism. If everything is a result of chance, then the theory itself is a result of chance, so why should I believe it?

This kind of circular nonsense is illustrated when someone makes a statement like 'All generalisations are false'. Now this can't possibly be true as a statement of fact. It has a 'self-destruct' notice written all over it. As soon as we examine this phrase, it explodes in our faces – if 'All generalisations are false', so is the generalisation that 'All generalisations are false'. Therefore, *all* generalisations are *not* false! Those who argue that we are just the result of a cosmic accident have to live with the tension of this illogicality all the time.

The other problem with believing we are here by accident is that it is also impractical. You can't live as though it were true because it would mean nothing really matters. Everything is the result of chance, so if my feelings and beliefs aren't based on anything dependable and don't have any real significance, I might just as well be committed to a fire extinguisher as to my wife! But who can live like this? We all need things of significance in our lives (like family, friends and work) to give our existence meaning. Life would be unbearable without them. If we are the result of a meaningless process, why do we cry out for meaning in our lives?

The Christian would argue that there is reason behind our existence and purpose for it. God created the human race – scientists can argue over how he did it – and gave guidelines for behaviour by way of the conscience and, of course, the Bible. God has given deeper significance to some things than others, so we just know that a fire extinguisher is not to be valued in the same way that our loved ones are. God wants us to enjoy his creation, respect our fellow humans and find real contentment in our lives. His goal for us is that we should receive his personal help to become like his Son – the perfect human. A pretty amazing goal!

All this gives real purpose to the Christian's life. Imagine a boat on a rough sea with dead engines, no captain, rudder or anchor. It would be blown about by the dictates of the wind, drifting at the whim of every passing current. Now imagine another boat in an equally bad storm. This boat has engine power and all its crew and equipment, plus a variety of maps and charts. This boat is going somewhere. Christians are glad to be in this second boat, and maintain that their choice is both logically consistent and practically workable. They would need some pretty compelling reasons to abandon their views.

While we are pondering the meaning of life, we ought to think too about death. This is a frightening subject for many people, some of whom refuse to discuss it or hide their embarrassment by making a joke of it. Actor Woody Allen speaks for many of us when he says, 'I'm not afraid to die. I just don't want to be there when it happens!' Death is life's final mystery, and we are going to need more than clever theories to face it with confidence. Christians know that Jesus defeated death and has guaranteed a life of security and joy for them beyond the grave. Death becomes not an end but a beginning, not a brick wall but a doorway into another room. This is exactly what Jesus promised his followers:

> Don't be worried and upset . . . There are many rooms in my Father's house. I wouldn't tell you this, unless it was true. I am going to prepare a place for each of you. (John 14:1,2)

I have seen this theory working out in practice. I have conducted dozens of funerals, sat at lots of bedsides with dying people, spent hours counselling those who have been left behind. When the dying person was a committed Christian, the whole experience is different. Of course, there is sadness, anger, emptiness and all the other symptoms of grief; but there is also an extra dimension present. It is almost impossible to explain, but there is hope, peace, even an element of joy in a truly Christian funeral. When there is no faith, these elements are absent and the whole process of grieving, and the funeral service itself, has a deep futility and hopelessness about it.

This is an issue we dare not make a mistake about. The most certain statistic of all is that one out of every one person dies! Have we got a philosophy of life that can cope with death – our own death and of those closest to us? Put coldly and a little cruelly, will our beliefs stand up to the sight of a loved one's corpse on a hospital bed, a child's coffin being carried into church, or a parent's casket disappearing for the last time behind the crematorium curtain? No one should answer 'Yes' to that question without careful thought. I have known convinced atheists ask for God's help to cope with the loss of their partner, and others who have been angry at God for taking away someone they loved – all of them not realising the absurdity of being angry with – or asking for the help of – someone you don't believe exists!

In the face of the fact of death, most people simply look the other way and hope for the best. This is a strange response to life's most crucial question. We prepare financially by taking out insurance and making a will; but we prepare spiritually by indulging in wishful thinking! Our eternal destiny deserves much more serious attention, and not just as a sterile academic exercise but as a vital issue which affects us all. Those who come to terms with their own death stand a much greater chance of coming to terms with life. Most of us view death as going from the land of the living to the land of the dead. Christians have a marvellous assurance of a heaven in which all tears are wiped away, and perfect rest and joy continue for ever. They are going from the land of the dying to the land of the living!

This chapter has attempted to look seriously at three very important questions – our sense of right and wrong, problems in the world, and the meaning of life. The Christian answers are perfectly rational. In 2000 years, no one has come up with anything close to Christianity's practical, consistent world-view. No wonder Christians hold their views so passionately. They make sense and they work.

11

The final crunch

'I've made my mind up. Don't confuse me with the facts!'

Many of us act like this even if we don't use these precise words. They explain why plenty of people are not Christians. The evidence in favour of Jesus Christ and his message is very strong indeed. The purpose of this book has been to show how compelling the facts really are. Sadly, few people make decisions on the basis of facts! Most of us operate at the level of feelings. Millions continue to smoke despite clear evidence that it damages health. A similar number overeat and take no exercise, even though the problems associated with this kind of lifestyle are well known. And even if you are a non-smoking, fibre-eating fitness fanatic, you are still not safe! Examining our behaviour carefully, almost all of us will find that we make some decisions and adopt a certain lifestyle on the basis of something other than the true facts. Personal pleasure, upbringing, tradition and a variety of other feelings and assumptions influence us strongly.

This means that it is perfectly possible to read all the way through a book like this and be convinced that it makes a lot of sense. You can see the logic of the arguments. You agree that there is a great deal of evidence to support real Christianity. *And you are probably not going to do anything about it!*

This is for the same reason that the 40-a-day man puffs himself to an early grave. He knows the facts about smoking but doesn't want to, or feels he can't, change. Even if the facts are forcefully and clearly outlined in a brilliantly creative video presentation accompanied by glossy brochures, we will only have succeeded in making our heavy smoker a superbly well-informed, perhaps slightly more miserable, heavy smoker! Only when he *wants* to change are we going to see any real action.

So, why don't people who can see a lot of sense in Christianity want to become Christians? Here are five significant reasons:

1. Comfort

They can't be bothered – they are much too comfortable to be disturbed. It's as simple as that. It would be too much effort to change, too much of an upheaval in their lives. These people have a sleeping sickness in their souls. They are permanently in the twilight zone between waking and sleeping, when the last thing they want to do is move!

But the fact is, such people are in great danger. When doing experiments on frogs, scientists discovered that if you throw a frog into boiling water, it leaps out promptly. If, however, you place a frog in cold water and gradually heat it up, you can boil it alive before it realises what's happening! Many people are in a similar predicament. They are being lulled into a false sense of security, tragically unaware of the danger they are in. Too comfortable.

Our relative affluence in the West doesn't help our apathy. Full stomachs, warm homes and comparative security tend to dull our senses to life's crucial questions. We are exposed to endless trivial distractions – television, videos, hobbies, and all kinds of other leisure pursuits. These activities, while not wrong in themselves, can create an environment in which our minds are permanently cushioned against serious thought. The trouble is, 'comfortable' may not mean 'safe'. Suppose you are on a luxury liner in one of the plushest suites with sumptuous furnishings and delicious food, everything your little heart desires. This is the life! The trouble is, the ship is the *Titanic!* You may be very comfortable, but you are in danger. Every human being is on a collision course with God: we have all failed to obey

his laws and abide by his rules. Christianity provides a life-boat, an escape from the anger God feels towards the wrong in our lives. Jesus died in our place to give us this escape route. All other escape routes are dead ends.

However satisfied we may feel, *if Christianity is true we are in desperate danger*. Remember, the *Titanic* was supposed to be unsinkable!

2. Cowardice

Many people don't become real Christians because they haven't got what it takes. Guts! They are too concerned that people might say they have 'got religion', 'joined the God squad' or generally taken leave of their senses. Christianity is hardly fashionable and certainly not the kind of thing any self-respecting trendy would want to admit to. This is often true of the so-called rebellious younger generation. They may want to rebel against an older generation's values, but they are just as terrified of being out of step with their mates as anyone else. This is one of the reasons why, no matter which British town you happen to be in, the youngsters tend to dress the same! For all of us there is at least one group of people we are determined to please.

On my first day at secondary school, I turned up looking cherubic in my new uniform. The only problem was I had been sold the wrong tie by a careless shop assistant! I was teased mercilessly about it and spent most of the day with my head bowed as if in prayer. To make matters worse, the tie I had been sold belonged to one of our great rival schools! I hated being the odd one out, ridiculed and laughed at.

Most of us can relate to this. We think the people at work, the lads in the pub, the friends at the club and members of the family will all think us very weird if we suddenly announce that we have become Christians. We don't want to be out of step with everyone else. We want to be accepted and well thought of. And there is pressure from wider society too. Anybody who is over-enthusiastic about anything – politics, conservation, religion – is labelled a fanatic. The emphasis today is on 'live and let live', 'take it easy', 'relax'. We are becoming so laid back, we are close to being laid out! In addition, cynicism is rampant, and negative destructive humour is the order of the day. We have become so sophisticated that we can poke fun at everything. In this atmosphere, passionate commitment to anything is difficult, and commitment to Christianity, with its old-fashioned image, almost impossible. Many people are afraid to become Christians because they fear rejection from friends, and because society puts subtle pressure on them to appear sophisticated and chic.

All of which means we have to stop all this rubbish about Christianity being a soft option, something for those who can't handle life in their own strength! It is tough being a Christian, so tough there isn't much of it about. Any fool can mock

Christianity, but it takes real courage to become a follower of Jesus Christ.

Of course the cynics will ridicule. They know the price of everything and the value of nothing. But behind the mask of twentieth-century sophistication are disfigured and tear-stained faces. No hope here, no lasting joy, no comfort, nothing to sustain during times of tragedy. How many promises the smiling eyes of the mask seem to offer! How little fulfilment! Early pop idol Cliff Richard made this discovery for himself some years ago:

> It was a few years into my show business career when I first sensed a sort of incompleteness. I don't know how else to put it. It was as though there was something more to life, despite the fact that I had so much going for me. Certainly as much fame, fortune and popularity as any one person could handle. The girls screamed, hits came regularly, accountants were employed to cope with the income, but, despite all that, it didn't add up to satisfaction. When I went home and took off the public mask, which I guess we all wear some of the time, I still had to live with the real me. And although I don't suppose I was any worse – or any better, come to that – than the next bloke, I knew that success, fans and money were no compensation for being restless deep within myself. (Cliff Richard, *Mine to Share*, Hodder.)

3. Cost

What will I have to give up if I become a Christian?

Most people have a worry that becoming a Christian will involve them in not doing all the things they enjoy doing. Well, there is no getting away from the fact that Christianity is costly. It cost God's Son his life, and it's not going to cost us any less. We probably won't be called on to die physically for our faith – though some are – but we will be called on to 'die' to everything God doesn't want us to be. Being a Christian costs everything. You are not your own boss any more. What *God* wants is now more important than what *you* want.

All this can seem pretty terrifying until you examine what it is you are being called on to do. From the outside it looks like a raw deal: 'Give up wine, women (or Chippendale men) and song, and Christianity will give you stewed tea, frumps (or wimps) and hymns!' No wonder the price of Christianity seems high. But this caricatured comparison misses the point. Why?

First, we get something permanent to replace the temporary. The good feelings we get from the new gadget at home, our participation in sport, a favourite TV programme, are all passing pleasures; they are not going to last. Christianity offers something that cannot be pushed out by the latest craze, replaced by any change in fashion, be made obsolete by any development in technology or be terminated by death! It puts the cost into perspective when you realise that you will be giving up what you can't keep in order to accept what you can't lose.

Second, all other satisfactions are cheap imitations. Why be satisfied with a print when you can have the original? It is very hard to explain this without sounding arrogant. Sometimes when I talk to people who are not Christians, I am amazed at how little it takes to please them. What they describe as exciting appears to me to be unsatisfying and flat. Say a professor of mathematics was talking to a six-year-old about arithmetic. The professor would find it impossible to limit his thinking to addition and subtraction when he had tasted the delights of calculus and geometric progression! Of course, he would understand the boy's position because he had been at that stage once himself. But he would gain little joy in attempting 16–7 or 9+36. The boy, on the other hand, would think it a great accomplishment if he could solve these problems! If he saw some of the professor's work, it would look like a page filled with a jumble of meaningless shapes. He would dismiss it as silly or boring, not half as good as the real numbers he was working with.

In the same way, people who aren't Christians generally do not understand what real Christianity is all about and so tend to dismiss it. On the other hand, people who are Christians understand why those who aren't may find some things very pleasurable and difficult to give up, because before they became

Christians they used to have the same priorities. Since meeting Jesus, however, there is no way they could be satisfied with what seems to them now to be trivial pursuits!

4. The Church's image

TV personality Noel Edmonds said, 'The Church is the dullest experience that we have in this country.' This is one of the main reasons why people are put off Christianity. Television often portrays clergymen as fanatical bigots or wet, effeminate wimps who wouldn't harm a fly, or simply idiots. Church congregations seem to consist mainly of elderly women who meet in ancient buildings and participate in some obscure ritual that seems to involve little more than entering the building, singing a few old hymns and being asked to part with hard-earned money to help prevent the steeple falling down. A club with three rules – turn up, sing up and cough up!

Sadly, some churches are like this, but they are (thank God) a dying breed. The real Church is not a building but a people who have met Jesus. This Church is completely different from its sick image. The true Church of Jesus is growing rapidly. Every day 100,000 people are converted to Christianity! The only continent on which the church is not growing rapidly is Europe, but even here there are encouraging signs of life. I could take you to dozens of churches where the services are interesting, varied and exciting, and the atmosphere has to be experienced because it can't be explained. So don't be fooled by bad experiences you may have had, boring school assemblies, TV vicars or the crusty old fool who did your gran's funeral. Church need not be like this. In fact, a real church isn't.

It's also wise to remember when you go to a church for the first time that you aren't going to find everything happening the way you want it. Someone has said that there is no such thing as a perfect church and, if you did find one, you shouldn't join because you would spoil it! The Church is trying to do something pretty amazing – bring people from different generations and backgrounds together to form loving, active communities. I know few other institutions that are attempting to do the same. Being part of a church means being involved in a local community of believers, and you should always go with the intention of putting in as much as you get out of it.

5. The invisible enemy

Even if Christianity is true, the four obstacles I have outlined stand in the way of many people coming to accept the message for themselves. Comfort, cowardice, cost and the church's image can provide pretty strong opposition. But now I come to the greatest opposition of all: the invisible enemy. This opponent is incredibly dangerous for two reasons – it's immensely powerful and also a brilliant master of disguise. So superb is the disguise that most of the human race doesn't even realise it's there! This evil power operates on everyone, and its main job is to blind people to the truth about themselves and God. Christians believe that this power is an evil personality called Satan. He has conned most of humanity into believing that he is either a figure of fun with a pitchfork in his hand, or a figment of the imagination. Unfortunately, he is real. He operates just like a deadly virus. You can't see him but the damage he does is terrible.

Unless you are aware of this power at work you will never understand why a decision to follow Jesus Christ is so hard to make. *Somebody does not want you to make it.* Imagine making a decision to take up serious jogging, but every time you were getting changed into your trainers you were struck down by some kind of viral infection which made you very lethargic. It would take a massive effort of will to force your body out of the door and to start running.

Similarly, whenever people make a decision to examine the claims of Christianity seriously, Satan mobilises his forces to produce 'spiritual lethargy'. 'When you're a bit older,' he whispers, 'Remember your image – no one believes it any more', and so his deceits go on. This is usually enough to keep us away from the discovery of God. How easily we are deflected from our search for truth! These excuses are going to sound really lame when we come face to face with God. 'Oh, sorry, God. They told me you were dead. Anyway, I would have tried to find out about you but I was too busy. It just seemed irrelevant compared with following Manchester United!' All sounds pretty sick really. 'Too busy'? When the average person in Britain spends 26 hours a week watching the box! 'No one believes it any more'? When there are seven times as many people in church on Sunday as are watching football on Saturday! No, these excuses don't bear up to examination. Someone is conning us!

So what?

Single-minded people make it to the top in sport, politics and just about any other field. They have to be single-minded to cope with the great pressures that they are under. Linford Christie, former Olympic 100-metre champion had a coach, Ron Roddan, who helped him stay totally focused:

> I hated the cold nights, hated Ron at times, but I kept at it. I ran repetition 300 metres and 200 metres. I pulled heavy tyres along the sprint straight, and I began weight training. So it went on, day after day, week after week, right up until Christmas. Ron was kind; like Mr Scrooge he gave us Christmas Day off. (From *Linford Christie*, Arrow Books.)

No one doubts this commitment to winning. If only we displayed half the commitment in our search for truth, many more people would find it.

Do you really want to know the truth about yourself and your world? Do you really want to feel clean inside, set free from the mistakes of the past? Do you really want to experience life as God intended? If so, you need to consider the offer that Christianity makes very seriously. This will take time and real commitment, but the prize beats an Olympic Gold by miles!

So what now?

I am always very sceptical when I see books or articles with titles like 'Six Simple Steps to a Better Sex Life' or 'How to Earn a Million by a Week on Friday'! You know – the kind of book that reduces a massive area of expertise down to a few simplistic steps which fail to do the subject justice. I hope to avoid being so naive, but I want to give four steps that I believe can demonstrate to the honest enquirer the truth and power of Christianity.

1. Be bold

Have the guts to examine all the evidence honestly, even if it makes you very uncomfortable. The motto of the SAS, 'Who dares wins', is nowhere more relevant than in the search for truth. People may well want to know what's come over you. The search could easily be difficult! Be bold enough to keep on searching even if you don't appear to be getting anywhere. Reject the weakness of many in our society whose motto appears to be 'If at first you don't succeed – give up and try something else!'

Be strong enough to start the journey with as little excess baggage as possible. In other words, get rid of as many preconceptions and prejudices as you can. Don't decide Christianity is going to be false (or true) before you start. There are already too many people who make up their minds and then look round for facts to support their view; don't add to their number. If you can be ruthless enough with yourself, try to forget all you think you know about Christianity and approach the whole thing as if you'd never heard of it.

A great many important scientific discoveries have been made by using this 'clean sheet' principle. Ignoring what 'everybody knows', scientists have demonstrated the opposite to be true. Centuries ago 'everybody knew' that the earth was flat. The fact was that everybody was wrong and was shown to be wrong when brave men stood against them with the facts. Most of us have grown up in a world which has made similar statements about Christianity, conditioning us against it. 'Everybody knows that the Church is a dying institution.' 'Everybody knows that no intelligent person believes that stuff any more.' It is going to take a bold person to ignore what 'everybody knows' and examine the evidence on its merits.

2. Be clear

Be clear about what the Christian faith is not. It is not about stopping swearing, giving up chocolate for Lent or becoming a *Songs of Praise* devotee. The Christian message is that God exists; he caused the world to come into being and created human life; this humankind was given the freedom to follow God's laws or reject them; humankind chose to go its own way and has chosen to do so ever since; God, because he is loving, wanted to give his creatures another chance, so he came to earth as a man and took on himself the punishment for our rebellion; God then offered this second chance to everyone who would accept it as a free gift.

God's gift, when it is received, brings with it a guarantee of eternal happiness with him after death, forgiveness, peace and purpose on earth. The gift does not guarantee an easy life free from trouble – sometimes precisely the opposite. Receivers of the gift expect opposition from natural and supernatural enemies. They also enjoy a new strength and enter a dimension of living which would otherwise be unknown.

3. Be active

Say you wanted to find out about athletics. If you went to one race meeting as a spectator and then dismissed athletics as a waste of time, I'd say you weren't really that bothered in the first place. You couldn't possibly dismiss the fun of competing, the sense of achievement in participating and the thrill of winning on the strength of this one brief view from the stands. Being an athlete is not a spectator sport. Get out on the track and run, talk to some real athletes, chat to a coach, read some books on athletics and then decide if it is for you. So, if you really want to find out if Christianity is true . . .

Start doing things real Christians do!

- Get a Bible and begin to read the New Testament. Make sure you have a recent translation such as the Contemporary English Version (CEV) or the Good News Bible (GNB). Find a Christian bookshop and ask them to recommend one or two books that explain the Christian faith. If you find the Bible difficult to understand, they will have booklets that explain it bit by bit.
- Go to a lively church. Ask questions about everything in the service you don't understand. (It's usually best to wait until the end to do this – most ministers aren't too happy with questions during the sermon!) Make an appointment to see one of the leaders. Be polite, but ask every awkward question about God that you really want to know the answer to. Don't try to ask clever questions just for the sake of an argument. A good leader will find it difficult to take you seriously if you do.

  Go to church regularly for a number of months. Keep asking questions. Keep asking yourself, 'Is this real? Is anything happening to me? Is it true?' (If you can't find a lively church near you, write to or phone the Evangelical Alliance and ask if they can tell you of one locally; their address is The Evangelical Alliance, Whitefield House, 186 Kennington Park Road, London SE11 4BT, telephone 020 7207 2100, email london@eauk.org)
- Start to pray. At first it will feel very odd talking into what seems like empty space, but it does get easier. You might want to start by praying something like this:

  'God, I'm not even sure that you are there. But if you are, I want to find out the truth about you. Please show yourself to me so that I can find out for myself what you are really like.'

A prayer like this confirms that you are serious in your search. Don't try to use religious language or pretend to be holy or pious. God already knows you aren't! Just talk as naturally as possible.

Be changed!

None of these steps will make you a Christian. They are stages along the road to discovery. Ultimately, being a Christian involves a relationship, a growing friendship with Jesus as a person, an experience of his love and power. This encounter with the living God is what real Christianity is all about. Don't settle for anything less. Don't settle for anything else. Don't settle – search! Then you will discover the truth of his promise for yourself:

> You will turn back to me and ask for help, and I will answer your prayers. You will worship me with all your heart, and I will be with you . . .
>
> (Jeremiah 29:12,13)

To find out more . . .

Basic Christianity, John Stott, InterVarsity Press

Mere Christianity, C S Lewis, Fount, an imprint of HarperCollins, 1983

Evidence that Demands a Verdict (2 volumes, 1990), *Christianity: A Ready Defence* (1991), *Answers to Tough Questions* (1989), all by Josh McDowell, Scripture Press

Questions of Life (1993), *Searching Issues* (1994), *Why Jesus?* (1991), all by Nicky Gumbel, Kingsway

Can Man Live Without God?, Ravi Zacharias, Word Publishing, 1994

The Bible: Fact or Fantasy?, John Drane, Lion Publishing

The Search for God: Can Science Help?, John Houghton, Lion Publishing

A Guide to Science and Belief, Michael Poole, Lion Publishing

Get into the habit . . .

If you would like to explore making regular Bible reading part of your life, Scripture Union invites you to **request free samples** from a range of personal Bible reading guides:

CLOSER TO GOD – experiential, relational, radical and dynamic, this publication takes a creative and reflective approach to Bible reading with an emphasis on renewal.

DAILY BREAD – aims to help you enjoy, explore and apply the Bible. Practical comments relate the Bible to everyday life, combined with information and meditation panels to give deeper understanding.

ENCOUNTER WITH GOD – provides a thought-provoking, in-depth approach to Bible reading, relating Biblical truth to contemporary issues. The writers are experienced Bible teachers, often well known.

SU also produces Bible reading notes for children, teens and young adults. They are available from any Christian bookshop. For information:

- phone SU's mail order line: 0845 07 06 006
- email mailorder@scriptureunion.org.uk
- fax 01908 856020
- log on to www.scriptureunion.org.uk
- write to SU Mail Order, PO Box 5148, Milton Keynes MLO, MK2 2YX

Also recommended:
CLOSER TO GOD FOR NEWCOMERS: MEET THE REAL JESUS by Belinda Pollard offers an encounter with Jesus through the Bible. Forty brief excerpts taken from Luke's Gospel and the Book of Acts, with helpful insights. It describes Jesus' life and the effect he had on the people he met.
ISBN 1 85999 459 8

And other books from Stephen Gaukroger, also available from Scripture Union:

FIRST STEPS: A practical and inspirational book to hold your hand through the vital early days of being a Christian. With 10 session outlines for small groups.
ISBN 1 84427 070 X
BEING BAPTISED: An essential and accessible book for anyone curious about or considering believer's baptism as a part of their journey of growing faith.
ISBN 1 85999 768 6

Scripture Union
USING THE BIBLE TO INSPIRE CHILDREN, YOUNG PEOPLE AND ADULTS TO KNOW GOD